THE BEST
WOMEN'S STAGE
MONOLOGUES
OF 1990

JOCELYN BEARD has edited <u>Contemporary Movie Monologues: A Sourcebook for Actors</u> (Fawcett/Columbine, Spring 1991) and <u>Comedy Monologues: A Sourcebook for Actors</u> (Fawcett/Columbine, Winter 1991).

WILLIAM ESPER has taught acting for over 25 years in his New York Studio and is a full professor and Head of the Professional Actor Training Programs at Rutgers University's Mason Gross School of the Arts.

ii

THE BEST WOMEN'S STAGE MONOLOGUES OF 1990

Edited By
Jocelyn Beard

SK
A Smith and Kraus Book

A Smith and Kraus Book
Published by Smith and Kraus, Inc.

Copyright © 1990 by Smith and Kraus, Inc.
All rights reserved

CAUTION: Professionals and amateurs are hereby warned that the plays represented in this book are subject to a royalty. They are fully protected under the copyright laws of the United States of America, and of all countries covered by the International Copyright Union (including the Dominion of Canada and the rest of the British Commonwealth), and of all countries covered by the Pan-American Copyright Convention and the Universal Copyright Convention, and of all countries with which the United States has reciprocal copyright relations. All rights, including professional, amateur, motion picture, recitation, lecturing public reading, radio broadcasting, television, video or sound taping, all other forms of mechanical or electronic reproduction, such as information storage and retrieval systems and photocopying, and the rights of translation into foreign languages, are strictly reserved. Particular emphasis is laid upon the question of readings, permission for which must be secured from the author's agent in writing.

Pages 81-85 constitute an extension of this copyright page.

Library of Congress Catalog Card Number: 90-91799

ISBN: 0-9622722-1-3

Cover design by David Wise
Text design by Jeannette Champagne

Manufactured on recycled paper in the United States of America

First Edition: January 1991
10 9 8 7 6 5 4

Smith and Kraus, Inc.
Main Street, P.O. Box 10
Newbury, Vermont 05051
(802) 866-5423

Quality Printing and binding by Eagle Printing Co., Inc.
Albany, New York 12202, U.S.A

ACKNOWLEDGMENTS

Grateful thanks to the playwrights for their extraordinary talent.

CONTENTS

CONTENTS

CONTENTS

FOREWORD

The 1990 theatrical season has been particularly kind to actresses. Intriguing, desirable women's roles have been well-crafted by an eclectic mix of playwrights, creating new opportunities for actresses to explore the medium without fear of repeating the same old themes that have been haunting women's monologues for years and years.

No more lovely Lauras, Stand-By-Your-Man Stellas, or jaundiced Juliets! This year we meet a new breed of woman like the fierce-minded Miriam who is driven by grief to self-mutilation in "Miriam's Flowers" by Migdalia Cruz or the indomitable Mary Lou Anderson, a farm girl from the midwest who teaches cannibals of New Guinea how to prepare a proper Thanksgiving turkey in Josh Manheimer's hysterically funny, "Kuru." Women of great strength, like Laura, a black woman struggling to hold onto her family's farm in Samm-Art Williams' "Woman From The Town" and women of great weakness, like the emotionally confused Rosannah of "Brilliant Traces" by Cindy Lou Johnson are but samples of the characters awaiting you within. Open, read and enjoy!

--Jocelyn Beard
Patterson, NY
August, 1990

INTRODUCTION

Each day that I head into my New York Studio to teach I am certain that two things will happen: there will be a long delay at the Lincoln Tunnel and during the course of the day at least two students will ask if I know of a good monologue. This request is often tinged with a note of desperation because within the week, the actor has an audition for this or that agent, or the New York Shakespeare Festival, or some other equally important opportunity. I am often astonished, how young actors will work assiduously for months to obtain an audition and then scramble about at the last moment to look for suitable material.

Every actor when he ventures on the perilous seas of a professional career should be equipped with talent, excellent training, a good headshot and an extensive number of wonderful monologues.

At the Professional Actor Training Program at Rutgers University's Mason Gross School of the Arts we consider monologues so important that we require the actors to begin their search for them a full year before our New York Showcase and their graduation. We allow this much time because we know that monologues help get actors representation and jobs! We also know that finding them is no easy task. Every actor in the Professional Acting Program is required to have at least 6 or 7 pieces in his monologue repertoire. Experience tells us it is important that an actor have more than one or two pieces prepared for presentation.

One colleague of mine who directs constantly for theatres across America told me he finds nothing so frustrating than to find himself interested in an actor at an audition, and out of that interest; to ask the actor if he can do something else only to be told "No, I'm sorry, that's all I have prepared". I have shared this experience often when I am auditioning for the program at Mason Gross or at my New York Studio. Sometimes the chosen material does not give me a deep enough insight into the actor's personality or the pieces are too much alike. But something about the actor appeals to me and I want to get a more extensive insight into a particular persons temperament and personality. I always warm to the actor who responds with an emphatic "yes" when he is asked to do another

INTRODUCTION

piece. One actor I trained called me to share the news that he had just signed with a prestigious agency. "I was so glad I was prepared", he said. "They kept asking me if I had another monologue and after I did the seventh they agreed that they wanted me to be their client".

Good monologues effectively performed can open many doors for the actor. Finding pieces that are really right for you, that the person holding the audition has not seen many times before is not easy. It is much better to present material that is fresh and unfamiliar because then the auditioners can look at you without being reminded of all the other actors that they have seen present the same monologue. For people who see many auditions, nothing is as refreshing as a new piece of material they have not seen before. The choice of material alone can immediately put you on the casting persons good side or alienate them from you.

The editor of this collection understands the above point very well. What follows is a wonderful collection of brand new material. Not one monologue in this collection will elicit a groan upon its announcement. And wonder of wonders, all of this material is for women! Really good monologue material for women seems always in short supply. Even though we have seen the emergence of some wonderful women writers there is still a large imbalance between good material for men and for women. Every actress should be heartened and inspired by this rich and varied collection of material.

Here are women of every age, race, economic background and temperament. Not only that but much of the material is as current and fresh as todays newspaper. The topics range over issues such as: our polluted environment in A Murder of Crows, child abuse in Mark Dunn's Belles, life in a welfare hotel in Jimmy Breslin's Queen of the Leaky Roof Circuit. There are also lots of amusing speeches from ladies in Vital Signs, At The Still Point and Search and Destroy and many touching, delicate speeches from women like Joanna in Elliot Loves, or Delfina in Miriam's Flowers.

In looking for speeches to use for auditions, look first to

INTRODUCTION

your own inner response to the material when you first read it. Does something about it rouse you inside? Does it make you laugh or cry with outrage? If so, you may be on the track of something really good. If you can easily identify with the human content of the speech and the woman who is speaking you will be well on your way to making a marriage between yourself and the character. This can only result in an effective performance.

Good monologues stand entirely on their own, almost as if they were miniature one act plays with their own beginning, middle and end. They must have impact. They should make us smile (if not laugh out loud) or touch us or best of all amaze us. As with any piece of acting, there are certain questions which must be answered as you begin work on a chosen speech. Most importantly, where am I, whom am I talking to, and what do I need to accomplish with the speech and why? Remember, the person you are talking to may not necessarily be the character in the play. It may be anyone who seems to you logical, and gives you a need to reveal the content of that speech to them. Monologues for auditions create some very special problems for the actor. One is, the person you are addressing isn't there! You must create them for yourself and for the viewer. That means creating their emotional reality for you. Is it someone you loathe, or love, or a total stranger? Just as in an on-stage phone conversation you must imagine their responses and react as if they were there in the flesh. Monologues make tremendous demands on the actor's imagination and truly take as much care and attention as a full fledged scene. That's why they are often so rewarding to work on. Especially, if their content is as human and true as the speeches in this book are.

Now that you are armed with an inviting array of speeches to choose from and sage advice for your preparation or their performance, I can only wish you good luck.

--William Esper

THE BEST
WOMEN'S STAGE
MONOLOGUES
OF 1990

AMULETS AGAINST THE DRAGON FORCES
by Paul Zindel

Mrs. Boyd - 40s-50s - Staten Island - 1955
Mrs. Boyd is a live-in nurse who has been hired by Mr. DiPardi
to care for his dying mother. When Mrs. Boyd and her son,
Chris, move into the DiPardi household, it soon becomes evident
that nothing is as it seems. Mrs. Boyd is revealed as an
unscrupulous woman who will pilfer from her employers and
take kickbacks from undertakers in order to save enough money
to buy a house for her and Chris. When she discovers that Mr.
DiPardi is a homosexual, however, she threatens to leave. Mr.
DiPardi begs her to stay, for he is desperate to have care for his
mother. As they discuss their differences, Mrs. Boyd lapses into
the story of her ex-husband's infidelity.

MRS. BOYD: Well, maybe once you were just as trusting and
believed that life was worth living...and that you were a part of it.
But something happened. Something was done to me. This will
probably give you a big laugh.
[FLOYD: I won't laugh.]
MRS. BOYD: My husband was transferred to a Manhattan precinct,
and so every morning he would have to leave earlier and ride the
ferry across New York Harbor. And every night he would drift
back. Drifting away and back, away and back, while I still clipped
recipes and planted lilies of the valley, and showed picture books to
my son. And then came the moment when it all changed. I think
that's how all things change--in a single moment. Like death, I
suppose. One moment you're alive, and the next you have death.
And my husband laughed about this one moment. He laughed at our
dinner table when he remembered something that had happened at
work, and he wanted to share it with me. He had been in his
uniform at a bar on Minetta Lane, he told me, when a young woman
noticed him and said, "Excuse me, officer, but you wouldn't give a
poor little girl a ticket for parking too long on a bar stool, would
you?" He had so enjoyed that remark he just had to share it with
me. And I think that moment when he was in that bar was the exact

1

second my life changed for me--and I wasn't even there! I didn't know how much had changed until months later when the wife of our family doctor called, Dr. Scala's wife was on the phone telling me not to let my husband touch me because he had contracted a somewhat rampant case of syphilis. Little Chris and I had been listening to the radio, to Kate Smith and then the Longine Symphonette, and a moment later the phone had rung and Dr. Scala's wife told me not to let my husband near me until she would notify me of an "all-clear." For me, that was the moment I went crazy...because my best lady friends and all the glossies had told me to go crazy. They said I should go mad, and not forgive. The tradition was quite clear. Syphilis and cheating were unforgivable! So I did not forgive, and I lost my husband, my son's father, our stucco home, and then all my friends--because they were still married, and I became the desperate divorcee. And my husband-- well, he drifted off permanently with the same young lady who had asked if she'd get a ticket for parking too long on a bar stool. That was just twelve, thirteen years ago. I had done what I was supposed to do. And now, the same glossies, the magazines, everyone is beginning to tell me I was wrong. Now I'm told perhaps I should have forgiven and forgotten and been supportive to my husband. I should have stood by him. Been sort of an adoring penicillin assist, I suppose. My husband still hates me. He thinks I'm the one who ruined our lives. *(She takes a sip of the drink.)* He blames me for Chris. For the dolls, the puppets, the need he has to perform and be liked. He blamed me for the fact that Chris used to imitate Carmen Miranda--the Brazilian star who did sambas with large bananas on her head--which I know is unbearably threadbare--but even I have considered that it was Carmen Miranda who single-handedly destroyed a vast section of American manhood--but I must tell you...that Chris used to watch me listening to Carmen Miranda, and when he saw me laughing and dancing to the records, he would look at her pictures on my albums and put on shows, and I laughed. I thought it was funny. He would wear bananas on his head, an eight-year-old boy with bananas on his head...

A MURDER OF CROWS
by Ed Graczyk

Jennie Woodson - 60s-70s - Ohio - Present
Jennie and Harley Woodson are an elderly couple faced with the
grim task of evacuating their Ohio farm. The forced evacuation
is the result of the discovery of an illegal toxic waste dump on
their land. Here, Jennie details the poisoning of her town.

JENNIE: There's more truth to superstition than most folks care to
admit, you know...Three times the murder circled...wide circles
over the whole village. It was a sign. You would have to have been
blind not to recognize it. I looked around to find a reason for their
peculiar behavior, and way off there down Cemetery Road...*(She
points out the exact spot.)* was coming a truck...a truck all loaded-
down with metal barrels headed for our old farmstead up there on
the hill. Once, sometimes twice a week after that, another truck
would come up the road. Each time the crows squawked and
circled. One day things started to become sick...Clyde Watkins'
bull, Cyrus Gilmore's chickens...Cyrus Gilmore, the Lord rest his
soul...and then, Harley. Folks were coming down with sicknesses
none of us had ever heard of before, with words as long as your
arm. It turns out they were all just a lot of fancy names for cancer,
anyhow. *(She fishes in her apron pocket for a wadded-up Kleenex.)*
One day, another truck came up Cemetery Road, there...full of men
dressed-up like those astronauts that went up to the moon. They
prowled around the fields and gardens digging up dirt and carrying
it away with them in jars. That was August tenth, I remember...I
was putting-up butter beans. The crows squawked and circled for
hours. The next thing we all knew they'd come back and put these
signs up all over the place...like the circus was coming to town.
(picking up the cabbage) Today, it's October...tomorrow, the tenth
again. I should be getting the cabbage ready for kraut. *(A tear
escapes. She wipes it away with her Kleenex.)* Good Lord, look at
me crying here over a shriveled-up old cabbage. Have you ever
heard of anything so foolish in your life? I should be crying over

something worthwhile...like my poor furniture. *(She holds out her nearly disintegrated Kleenex.)* By the time I get around to crying over that, there won't be any Kleenex left. The only thing still holding it together is old tried-up tears.

APOCALYPTIC BUTTERFLIES
by Wendy MacLeod

Trudi - 20s-30s - Maine - Present
Muriel and Hank are a young couple whose marriage goes on the rocks after the birth of their first child. To escape the escalating tensions at home, Hank begins an affair with Trudi, a local girl who is no stranger to extramarital activities. Despite her numerous liaisons, Trudi is lonely, as she confesses to Hank in a motel room.

TRUDI: I'm getting lonely being with you. The more I'm with you the lonelier I get. That's not a good sign. If I were older and wiser, I'd take a walk. I'd go home, watch "Miami Vice" and feel good about myself. I'd remind myself how good I live without a man. I'd regain my equilibrium. Ever since I met you, my life's been imbalanced, it tips in the love and sex direction. I look at your skin and think I'm gonna have a nervous breakdown if I'm not allowed to touch that man's skin. I meet 10 billion other men a day but I see you, my heart has a little heart attack, I get wet down there. Now then.

5

APOCALYPTIC BUTTERFLIES
by Wendy MacLeod

Muriel - 20s-30s - Maine - Present
When Muriel discovers Hank's infidelity, she flies into a rage and decides to take her baby and leave. She tells Hank's mother of her plan to move to a city and live in a hotel room where everything is always clean.

MURIEL: I'm gonna be something. I'm not gonna waste my life in this mosquito pit.
[FRANCINE: What are you gonna be?]
MURIEL: Something. I'm gonna move to New York City and buy the right clothes. There'll be a sadness in me no man can touch. Ah, Francine you shoulda seen that motel. So clean I would like to a lived there and <u>conveniences</u>--Kleenexes coming out of the walls, little packages of mouthwash, Whispermint, like candy only good for you, in the shower a dispenser full of Eurobath with glycerine you can use it anywhere, hands, face, hair whatever, and on the T.V. a little paper tent, a questionnaire asking me was I satisfied, the first time in my life anyone ever asked me.

APPLES
by Ian Dury

Delilah - 20s-30s - London - Present
Delilah is a woman of much experience who has been caught in
a web of political scandal. Here she speaks bitterly about the
influence that men have had in her life.

DELILAH: Men. Bloody men have been after me since I was
fourteen.
And before that, the dirty buggers. Not all of them though;
some of them only wanted to look at me or be seen with me.
One lonely old buzzard bought me a Ferrari so we could
drive from Amsterdam to Brussels for lovely meals.
They paid for my company and they were always good
company, and some of them are my friends, but none of
them will help me now.
The ones I call the lovers, however freaked out they are, only
want to help themselves.
They say they like everything, but they don't really like
anything, and all they want is more.
They couldn't help me now; not one of them; not in any way.
Not even the mesmerized ones, and certainly not the jack-
the-lads. Nor the powerful ones or the weak ones, and
definitely not the man in the street. What have I done?
I've taken this nest-egg, and it's hatching into an alligator.
What am I going to do?
I wish I had a bloody friend.

AT THE STILL POINT
by Jordan Roberts

Beth - 40s - A Home on the Hudson River, NY - Present
Beth is the hostess of the party and is quite tipsy. When a
young gate crasher, Billy, arrives, she is delighted to learn that
he knows Joey, who was her first big crush, and lapses into a
humorous anecdote of their first kiss.

BETH: You know, the first-and last- time I ever got drunk was with
him. Am I really gonna tell you this? Oh, what the hell. Don't tell
him. I was sixteen. He was younger. Rod's weird, cute little
brother Joey. Very intense. Read Poetry. And drank. Which I
don't remember any of us doing, not yet. And one night he told me
at this movie theater where we were both seeing the show, that the
moon was gonna eclipse that night, and did I wanna go see it with
him. So, "yes", I do. And we drive, I drive, us to...Turchin's
Orchard.

We get there, he brings out this bottle of wine. Awful. I
mean, really, worse than awful wine, and we start drinking from this
bottle and waiting for the moon to disappear. Now, over the years,
he and I could never get it straight what happened next. But
someone started kissing the other one. I say it was him, but he says
it wasn't, but I'm very shy, I think, especially when I drink.
[SARAH: You've certainly demonstrated that this evening.]
[BILLY: Go on]
BETH: Okay. So. Someone is kissing someone at the start. But,
eventually, this part we agree on, we both got very into it. Shoot.
He said he was in Love. Such beautiful things he was saying: "The
starlight was coming out of my...ears". Beautiful stuff. And I was
kinda falling too. He was goofy. I kinda had a crush on Rod. We
were gonna get whipped. None of it mattered. I was hearing the
music. And we forgot all about the moon. We're kissing and
kissing, getting very sloppy with the wine. It felt "adult". Having
this...wine sort of flow out of our open mouths. Slobbering all over
each other. Disgusting. But Poetic. I was feeling like a movie star.
This, glamorous, amorous Starlet. And the more we kissed, the

8

more I felt like her. Him too. Leading man. Definitely. Close-up. And he wanted to touch my breasts. Which nobody had wanted to do before that. Or asked anyway. Didn't strike me as a necessarily _bad_ idea. So, I said sure. Why not!

This is the hard part. See, I didn't really have much of a bust yet. Not for lack of prayer. And there was no shortage in the family. Mom and Aunt Sue had killer knockers. But mine, it turned out, were to be a winter harvest. And somewhere before this...tete a tete in the orchid, I had begun to augment my shape. I was neither the first nor the last Bill, we all did it. But I...elaborated ever so subtly. Working--I believe--according to the time-clock Nature _ought_ to have been using, but _wasn't_. *(She uses one hand to "wrap" imaginary toilet paper around her other hand, then forms two balls)* This meant adding--prudently--a few more inches...well, hell, Feet! of toilet paper to the mounds as the months went by. *(beat)* Poor Joey. I must've forgotten. It wouldn't have been so bad if it hadn't been for the dripping wine and messiness and all. These gobs of wet, stringy toilet paper all over his fingers....Put us both off to heavy petting for years!

"The moonlight's coming out of your ears." *(laughs) (beat)* Remember "kissing"? Remember.....

AT THE STILL POINT
by Jordan Roberts

Sarah - 40s - New York - Present
At the same party we meet Sarah. Sarah is engaged to Joey's brother, Rod. Billy has traveled all the way to New York from the west to tell Rod of Joey's death from AIDS. Sarah is the only one at the party that Billy feels comfortable enough to tell the truth about Joey. Sarah is shocked and saddened by the news, and senses Billy's inner torment. To help him to be able to express his grief, she reveals some of her own fears for her future.

SARAH: I'm going to have a baby. That's today's news. Little toy hammers. And I want to get married. Someone...decent. Strong. A grown up. Do I? It's time. Seems all the more pressing now. Somehow. Isn't that absurd? After everything I've seen and done and tasted all these years...Bearing a Child Out of Wedlock seems intolerable. Turning.

This man beats his wife in my building. It's been going on awhile. We all do...something...when it happens. Call the police..The City. Yell..."Stop". Some...attempt. But today. I woke up, this afternoon, and there it was again. All this screaming, banging. "Let me go...let me go!!" Familiar. I walk out my door and down the stairs, following the screams. And the hall is full. People. All these voices. "Let her out. Open the goddamn door. Now!" All of us. And the wife is crying. And the man, inside, is shouting, "It's fucking PRIVATE. Leave us alone." And the super starts banging on the door, with this hammer that always hangs from his belt--this huge metal door, this tiny little toy hammer. And the noise got so loud. And from inside...we hear this other...voice. Small. Quiet. Child's voice. Up against the door. And she says. To us: "No. No. Go away. It is nothing. Please leave...us alone. This..is..my..home." So familiar.

My Daddy was a dragon too. And I loved him, and I protected him. That's what families do. Hide and hurt. Ancient History. But my dragons are still here. All day. All night. Turning. Turning. When will they fall off?

10

AUGUST SNOW
by Reynolds Price

Taw Avery - 20s - North Carolina - 1937
Taw Avery is a young woman who has learned some tough life
lessons in her childhood in the orphanage. Here she tells of a
dream in which she used those lessons to their best advantage on
her first day of teaching school.

TAW AVERY: Since I was an orphan so early in life, I taught
myself to avoid most dreams--dreams at night, good or bad. They
seemed one strain I could spare myself; and I honestly think, in all
these years, I've never had two dozen dreams--not to speak of. Neal
dreams like a dog by the stove when he's here, the rare nights I get
to guard his sleep. Last night though when I finally dozed, sad as
I was, I lived through a dream as real as day.

   I'd finished my teacher's diploma and was ready to save the
world around me, all children. What thrilled me was that--they were
all young and not too hard yet to help. I'd show them the main
thing an orphan knows--how to tuck your jaw and brave hails of pain
and come out strong as a good drayhorse or a rock-ribbed house on
a cliff by water.

   But once I entered my class the first day and trimmed my
pencil and faced the desks, I saw they'd given me twenty grown
men--all with straight sets of teeth. I prayed I was wrong, that I'd
got the wrong room. Still I said my name, and the oldest man at the
back of the room stood tall at last in a black serge suit and said
"Don't wait another minute to start. We've paid our way."

   I had a quick chill of fright that I'd fail; but then I thought
of the week they died--my mother and father, of Spanish flu--and I
knew I did have a big truth to tell, the main one to know.

   I opened my mouth and taught those grown men every last
fact an orphan needs and learns from the day she's left--courage and
trust and a craving for time. They listened too but hard as I looked
in all the rows, I never saw Neal.

AUGUST SNOW
by Reynolds Price

Genevieve Slappy - 20s - North Carolina - 1937
Taw and Neal Avery rent a room in a boarding house from their
friend Genevieve Slappy. Genevieve shares a memory of her
mother and of her strength on the night that she died.

GENEVIEVE: I'm the youngest property-owner I know--this whole
house is mine. Mother left it to me, when my brother Dillard and
his big family were jammed in a one-story matchbox on the hot side
of town. She hoped I would sit here, quiet--renting rooms the rest
of my life--and forget Wayne Watkins and the dream of marriage.

    I don't understand. She and my father were happy together
as any two ducks on a deep warm pond. Many times as a child I
woke in the night and heard them laughing in the dark down the
hall. But when my father died, Mother--young as she was--just
started shrinking day by day till the night she vanished.

    Or so I recall it. She never warned me off men or low-rated
love till the evening she left us. Then that night, in the back
bedroom, I took in her supper; and she said "Sit still while I tell you
what's true." I sat by her knees, and she said "Stop waiting by the
door like a dog." I said "Beg your pardon?" She shut her eyes and
waited and then said "I'll pardon you when you can stand alone."

    I'd been walking unaided from the age of ten months--it
bowed my knees slightly--and I reminded her of that. I also
mentioned how she'd leaned on Papa those twenty-eight good years.
She didn't give an inch but turned her face to the wall, the picture
she'd painted as a girl--of buffalo--and she said "Then I can't pardon
you tonight, can I?"

    I laughed "No ma'am. Wait till breakfast tomorrow." And
she died before day--leaving me all this, as I said: *(Gestures
around)* my life. So she hoped anyhow. She may yet prevail.

    It *is* a strong house--heartwood beams and floors.

BELLES
by Mark Dunn

Peggy - 40 - Memphis - Present

Peggy is the oldest of six sisters and struggles to keep the family together via the phone lines. During a particularly intense evening of round-robin calling among the sisters, Peggy receives an obscene phone call and treats the caller to a taste of her sharp wit.

PEGGY: Hello?...No. I don't think I would like that. I think it would hurt...No, I don't think I like the sound of that either. May I go now?...You know, you don't catch people in the best of moods when you call at three in the morning. Most people are in their deepest stage of sleep by three. Wouldn't you be a little impolite if somebody woke *you* from a deep sleep?...Why don't you try warm milk or counting sheep?...Yes, you could count those too, but I don't see how a parade of naked mamas is going to--...No, actually you didn't have the pleasure. I was wide awake. I'm an insomniac probably just like you except that when *I* can't sleep, I just wander around all night *alone*. I don't resort to calling people on the phone to describe how I'd like to-- You know, it takes an infantile mind to-...I said you were not very bright, little boy. Nor articulate. You've used that same word ten times already. *(Losing composure.)* You're a very lucky man, little boy. If you had made this call two years ago, my husband would have been on the extension. He would have been listening to how you wanted to do this and that to various parts of my anatomy and he would have come looking for you. No place would have been safe. He would have found you out and ripped your voice box right out of your throat. Then you'd have to translate your filthy fantasies into sign language. And you know what? Sign language doesn't go over too well on the telephone. *(Answering a question.)* He died, you little creep. He got sick and died. It was the only battle he ever--*(She stops herself.)* I have some advice for you, little boy. Go into mommy and daddy's medicine cabinet and find the sleeping pills. Count out forty. Swallow. Pleasant dreams.

BELLES
by Mark Dunn

Aneece - 30s - Philadelphia - Present
Aneece has moved as far away from her hometown in Tennessee as possible in an effort to escape her mother and sisters. She is haunted by events in her past, however, and here imagines a phone conversation with her mother, with whom she hasn't spoken in many years.

ANEECE: Hello? Is that you, Mama? Your voice is quivering. You sound frightened. I'm afraid too, Mama. Of different things. Of noises in the middle of the night. Of being--You used to call me the antisocial daughter. Remember? "Why, here's the girls," you would announce to your friends. "There's Roseanne with the sad brown eyes, and Audrey so proud of her little curtsy. And there hiding behind the sofa is Aneece. She's anti-social, you see." Well, the label stuck, Mama. I'm the loner, doing everything my own way. When things click I come home, pat myself on the back and share my success with a bottle. And when my days *don't* go so well, the bottle's still there to comfort me. *(A beat.)* For a while at least. *(She takes a long drag of the cigarette.)* I hate it all, Mama. You can't possibly know what this feels like. But you *do* know what it's like to be afraid. You've lived through so many sleepless nights waiting for Daddy to come home--listening for him to unlock that back door. If it seemed like an eternity it meant he was having trouble with the key and the lock. And we all knew what *that* meant--Daddy was too far gone for anything but blind drunken rage. You used to pray out loud, Mama. I could hear you. Roseanne would cover her ears and Peggy would be locked in the bathroom with Audrey, but I could hear every word. You'd pray to God that for this one night Daddy would walk right up to the door, put the key in the lock and lumber in like a man who'd just had a few beers and was ready to sleep it off. I can still hear him at the back door, Mama. And I can still hear the prayers--"Our Father Who art in Heaven, don't let him kill us tonight." *(She takes another long drag, thinking.)* Now years later, alone in my apartment I can still hear him at the door. And I'm still afraid. *(Pause.)* I want to mend things with you, Mama. I want to wipe the slate clean. Maybe we can start talking each other through a few of these nights--scaring away the phantoms with the sound of our voices. *(THUNDER.)* I hear the thunder too, Mama. You better go. Call me again some time. I'd almost forgotten what your voice sounded like.

BRILLIANT TRACES
by Cindy Lou Johnson

Rosannah - 20s - Alaska - Present

Rosannah is a confused young woman who leaves her fiance at the altar, jumps into her car and then drives as far as she can before a blizzard forces her to seek refuge in the converted barn occupied by Henry Harry, a young man who has been wounded by life. The two slowly reveal insights into their inner torments as the storm continues to rage outside. Rosannah is greatly affected by Henry Harry's pain. In an attempt to comfort him, she reveals her own personal demons which manifest as feelings of alienation and loneliness.

ROSANNAH: Did you ever think that one time, a long time ago, when you were a little child, you were visited by extraterrestrials? They say that when you are visited by an extraterrestrial--after the visit, the extraterrestrial puts this spell on you so you cannot remember the encounter at all, and you wake up only with this sad kind of longing for something, but you don't know what. And you carry that sad longing with you all the rest of your life. And they say that if, by chance, you get hypnotized, then you reveal the encounter, under hypnosis and when you wake up, you remember it, and then, it is no longer a sad longing, but a real thing, which you know about, and even if people think you're crazy, talking all the time about your extraterrestrial encounter, that's ok, because in your heart you know what it was that had been locked up for so long and you are greatly relieved. *(Beat.)* I have often wondered what it would feel like to be greatly relieved. *(She rises and approaches Henry Harry standing closer, but still unable to touch him.)* I am not a very healthy person as I have said. I am, at this point in my life, relying on the long shot. I have really truly reached a point where I almost have expectations that an extraterrestrial will come to me. That I will see him and feel connected to him--right away, and he will say, Yes! It was me! It was me who touched you. And I won't care if he is very small or if he is milky white. I won't care at all, if I just know he is the one. *(Beat.)* If I just know he is the one.

16

DEMON WINE
by Thomas Babe

Mary - 30s - New York - Present
Mary is a woman of a less than wholesome past who is currently
the mistress of a crime boss. Her brash wit catches the attention
of Jimmie, a man who has recently gone to work for the mob.
Mary has spent many nights in motel rooms and is quite an
expert on the Bible. Here, she expresses her admiration of
Biblical heroines.

MARY: I read the Bible, you know, Jimmie, when I was but little.
There were heroes therein, and ladies. Now, these were not
ordinary people, but they had grand times. First one of them would
conquer something and be resplendent in the armor and the sweat
and, also, the "many wounds on the body," as Father McGrath
would explain, and then they would repair to the tents pitched, as
Father McGrath further explained, "at the calm outworks of the male
encounter." Or like that. The redoubts of the battle. They'd settle
in and a woman was always waiting who got the old stink of the
battle off his body, and also, got his body, and was told the best
stories you ever heard in you life about how the battle *seemed*, rather
than how it really was, which I imagine was just pigshit and ugly.
But she was happy, Jimmie, and you know, sometimes, some of
these boys would even bring back the tablets of stone and say, Look,
I found some laws while I was fighting, and she'd say, Get out of
those stupid clothes. They'd sleep all night curled up, him saying,
I discovered the Thou Shalt Not Eat the Salad with the Dinner Fork,
and her saying, Button it, honey, I got to rise with the dawn and
meet Ruth in the corn, and he'd say, What? What's that? *(Pause.)*
You like my explanation as to how I come to my understanding of
life?

EACH DAY DIES WITH SLEEP
by José Rivera

Nelly - 20s-30s - New York - Present
Nelly is the only one of Augie's children who cares enough to
see that he gets safely in to bed every night. Despite her
father's efforts to keep her in thrall, she has fallen in love with
the handsome Johnny, who returns her love. When he tries to
make love to her in the house, she tells him that she can't.

NELLY: I can't have sex here. Have no bedroom here. Every
night, I wander. From room to room. Looking for pieces of floor
not covered by members of my big family or animal droppings. But
even in this house, its hundred rooms, I share space with somebody.
If I do fall asleep, can't rest. My different color eyes are always in
conflict and they keep me awake. *(Nelly stands up and walks
normally, though with some effort. Her speech is nearly flawless.)*
The blue eye hates the grey eye for something the grey eye did to
the blue eye when I was still a fetus floating like a little fish in my
mother's huge body. Floating there among the schools of unborn
brothers and sisters. Today, the fighting between my eyes gives me
headaches, Johnny, and prophetic dreams. *(She smiles at him.)*
Help me rest. I'll stop using you. I'll love you--fiercely--the rest
of my life.

ELLIOT LOVES
by Jules Feiffer

Joanna - 30s-40s - New York City - Present
The evening has ended in disaster for Elliot and Joanna, who
have returned to their own apartments. Elliot resents Joanna for
having so easily won over his friends and Joanna can't
understand his resentment. They argue over the phone and
Joanna is finally forced to reveal her fear of intimacy.

JOANNA: I don't know what there is left to do. We do understand
things differently. We do miss connections. I'm sure that's true.
You do with me all the time. I was arrogant enough to think I
didn't with you. You see, I am probably most of everything bad you
think of me. But my effect is not calculated. What you call a
"technique." It's not a technique. I have four brothers whom I
never mentioned and with whom I'm not in contact. I loved them
passionately as a child. I have no addresses for them and I worry,
what if I die, how will they know? And that's my only reason for
resuming contact: so that they will be informed when I die. I have
arranged a life that belongs to no one. I am not home, Elliot. You
asked about my children and our having sex in the next room. I
think they don't hear. I'm sure they don't hear. But until you
asked, the question never occurred to me. I live in this state--I don't
know how to describe it, guilt is a step up from where I am now--a
state of moral absenteeism. I want no encumbrances. I'm on loan
to my children, but only till they're old enough for me to run away
from. I have two close friends whom you will never meet, Fay and
Walter. They adore me and I adore them, and we are intimates and
they know nothing about me. I chose to like you because I thought--
this is cruel--I thought you were safe.
[ELLIOT: I'm safe all right.]
JOANNA: I thought I could keep you in bounds. I used to think it
was a love of freedom that motivated my bad judgements.
[ELLIOT: Am I a bad judgement?]
JOANNA: You are right to be angry. I am better with your friends

19

than I am with you. I am at my most devastating with strangers. It used to vex and astonish me how much better my mother was with my friends than with her own children. No, Elliot, my bad judgement was that I could contain you.

THE FILM SOCIETY
by Jon Robin Baitz

Nan Sinclair - 40s - South Africa - 1970
The tragedy of South Africa's system of Apartheid is reflected in the relationships among the white faculty of the Blenheim School for Boys in Natal Province. Nan's husband has recently been fired from his teaching position at Blenheim for inviting a black minister to a school function. Nan has assumed his classes and here rebukes her students for their shallow understanding of their country.

NAN: *(Addressing her class.)* When I asked for essays on the Zulus, I wasn't looking for detailed accounts of native laziness in your father's factory, Cleasby. Nor am I interested in your examination of native killing techniques. It's tired, and I'm tired of it. It's as if your Africa were some kind of Atlantis, with drums and spears. It's not the one we're in. *(pause)* I thought we might, then, try these essays again? Somehow de-mythologyzed, okay? I was thinking--as I was reading them--I was thinking back, remembering, because my family had a number of maids as I was growing up. And there was a blur, a period of faces, names--I can't connect, but there was Edna. And she had been with us for some years--this good-natured, virtually invisible friend. Whose life was actually far more complicated than ours. My father did nothing, really, There was a vastness of leisure time, a morass. *(pause)* And Edna has this husband who worked in the mines, whom she saw with less and less frequency over the years. My mother found his presence--his dusty, coarse skin--upsetting, even if he was only to spend the night in the little room in the back. He was never actually forbidden; it was a kind of subtle discouragement. And--it was the same with her children--who had been cast out to the grandmother's little squash-patch and mud-hut in Zululand...somewhere where everyone might be re-united at Christmas for a couple of days or so. Eventually, the circumstances of this thwarted, enslaved life, all the wretchedness, made functioning as a human being harder and harder. *(pause)* And of course, as it becomes harder to function as a human being, it makes being a good servant pretty much an impossibility. *(pause)* She became moody. Forgetting to bathe, becoming, finally, something of a darkness in our home. And as Edna's personality became that of a toast-burning hag, I started to develop an intense dislike for her. There was a point where my family's main source of bored, wintry amusement--the height of morbidity, finally, was to, over dinner, discuss the decline of Edna, discuss it, in fact, as she served. *(pause)* And, of course, she began to sour. Her human-ness became overwhelming, like meat left out far too long. And when the dimension of her life overtook our own, she was finally, simply sent away. *(pause)* And the next week, it began again, with a new servant. So really, I mean, this kind of Atlantis you describe, it hardly does credit to the real one, which has its own violence, its own terror, quite independent of Fox's Africa of guns and war. That Africa--denies what we are. Our own brand of callousness. Surely there have been lives that have meant something to you? And I would very much like to know about that. Do you understand this?

FLORIDA GIRLS
by Nancy Hasty

Eulene - 50s - Florida - Present
Eulene lives next door to the Van Helmes and tends to look on
the dark side of things. She has agreed to look after their house
when they go to visit their grandmother, and here wishes them
a "bon voyage" as only a true pessimist can.

EULENE: Well, Rogene, don't you worry about a thing! We're
going to take care of your house while you're gone. I wanted to
come over last night, but Roberta said "no-o-o-o, Eulene, it's too
late." What? You don't know? Your girls didn't tell you last
night? Christine? Dee Dee? Rogene!! Do you know what we saw-
-big as life--in your front yard? A MAN! About yea tall! Rogene,
he was prowling through your bushes! There he was peeking in
your picture window...the next minute, he's back at your front door!
And then he just disappeared around the corner of the house.

(Following Rogene around the kitchen:) So--we called
Sheriff Bob Tomlin. At first, well, you know how he is--"Eulene,
did you see Big Foot again, or was it the Hinney Boys?" I said,
"Sheriff Bob, this time it wasn't the Hinney Boys!!" After I gave
him a piece of my mind, he sent a cruiser out and we looked high
and we looked low. That's when the Deputy talked to your girls,
but they said they didn't see or hear a thing. I'll tell you one thing--
Eulene Henderson's getting a pistol and then we'll see what's what!!!

Anyway, I just came over here to tell you that we're going
to take care of your house while you're gone. We're going to work
relays by that window yonder if we have to. Don't thank me,
Rogene, that's what neighbors are for.

(She starts out, then turns back:) Ya'll just be care-r-r-r-ful
driving. Roberta heard on the radio this morning that a whole
family was killed right out here on Highway 85.

(To Christine:) Well, Christine, evidently their car
stalled...and then a big semi came up from around the corner and
just ran ALL NINE OF THEM OVER!!!!

(Glancing at her watch:) Well, I gotta go. So ya'll just go
on your vacation and have fun!

GAL BABY
by Sandra Deer

Gal Baby - 40s - A Small Georgia Town - Present
Gal Baby introduces herself to the audience. She is a beautiful
southern belle who is growing older and whose lifestyle is
threatened with collapse.

GAL BABY: Eternal bloomer. Aren't they magnificent? That's
almost a miracle I think. A rose that grows year-round. Ever
blooming. Never dying. I believe in miracles.
   *(She sees Mr. Le about to put fertilizer on the Eternal
Bloomers.)* Wait a minute, Mr. Le. That fertilizer is for the
summer roses. I don't use that on my Eternal Bloomers. Mr. Le,
I said don't use the Baa Baa Doo on the Eternal Bloomers.
   (Now to the audience, whose presence she just now notices.)
Hey! I'm Gal Baby Partain Summers. Of course, Gal Baby is not
my real name. My real name is Eleanor. For my grandmother.
But when I was born, it was during the war, and Daddy was
overseas, my grandfather--Amos Partain--sent Daddy a telegram, and
all it said was, "It's a Gal Baby. Stop." And I've been Gal Baby
ever since.
   I think when parents give a child a nickname like that, they
oughta keep in mind that children grow up, and what's cute when
you're five, can sound pretty silly when you're forty-five.
   Actually, I'm forty-eight. I know I don't look forty-eight.
And by the grace of God and Estee Lauder, I don't intend to look
forty-eight. Besides, Tommy says, "Gal, you're not getting older.
You're just getting softer, and Southern men like their women soft."
And I say, "Auh huh, Tommy. Soft in the head."
   Tommy's my husband. The first time I laid eyes on him, I
said to myself, "There he is, Gal Baby. The boy of your dreams."
I wanted that one. And I got him. My daddy always taught me, "If
you want it, you need it." When I was little and wanted something
ridiculous like binoculars, my mother would say, "Arthur, an eight
year-old child does not need binoculars." And Daddy would just

24

grin at me and say, "Honey, if you want it, you need it." That was his philosophy of life. I think it's a good one, and I've tried to pass it on to both my children. Mercedes, who's married and lives in Quitman, and Tommy Jr., who's at the Air Force Academy learning to be a pilot. We had another child. Little Kathy. But she died when she was a baby. That about broke Tommy's heart. But I don't want to dwell on sad things. This is a happy day. We're having a major party here tonight. Black tie. And I have probably the most important appointment of my career this morning. I'm in real estate. Mostly I show homes that are in the historic register. The past is definitely in, you know. People care about the past. Particularly people who have never had one.

That's something we Partains are not short of. A past. We've got plenty of that. My grandfather, Amos Partain, had three wives. Sequentially, of course. He wasn't a bigamist. One of them, my Aunt Carlotta's mother, was half Cherokee. Carlotta is very proud of her Indian blood. Grandaddy was not a handsome or dashing man, but women adored him. And you know why? Because he appreciated us. Old or young, rich or poor, there was no such thing as an ugly girl to Grandaddy. In his eyes, we were all Helen of Troy. Men like that are rare.

Amos Partain made it his life's work to restore Rose Park Plantation to its antebellum grandeur. That's it over there across the lake behind those pine trees. And when he got done, it was something. The parties they would have there during hunting season. Oh my. Dukes and duchesses, presidents of railroads. Orchestras playing and handsome couples waltzing across that ballroom like there was no tomorrow.

Course there was, and this is it. Not for public knowledge, but we would be willing to sell Rose Park. I have it on the market. What we call a closed listing.

GOD'S COUNTRY
by Steven Dietz

Actor Six - 20s - 1983-Present - Various Locations In The U.S. "God's Country" deals with the 1983 racketeering trail of members of The Order, a white supremist organization suspected, among other things, of being responsible for the murder of Denver disc jockey, Alan Berg. Throughout the course of the play, unnamed characters provide insight into the making of a white supremist. Here, a woman shares her memory of the day that JFK was shot, and we can see that protestant fundamentalism was already playing a large role in her life.

ACTOR SIX: When President John F. Kennedy was shot and killed, I was six years old. My Sunday school teacher was named Mr. Oswald. This confused me. I was confused because this man had shot the President, but was allowed to lead my Sunday school class in prayer. I thought someone would say something. I thought one of the parishioners would say: You know, since Mr. Oswald shot the President, perhaps he should not be on our payroll any longer. But he was there. John 3:16. John 3:16

He was always very nice during Sunday school. He had a soft voice and crooked teeth and he let us eat pretzels. He looked different than he did on television. As the next Sunday approached, I was worried because I hadn't learned the Bible passage I'd been assigned.   Instead, I was sitting on the floor of my parents' bedroom, holding my baby brother, watching television. I saw Mr. Oswald.   I saw Mr. Oswald being taken away in handcuffs.   I thought, maybe I won't have to learn my Bible passage. Then he got shot. I watched it. They said he was dead. I laid my baby brother on the bed and I learned my Bible passage by heart.

And the following Sunday, Mr. Oswald was there again, teaching us how to pray. Still no one said anything: You know, since Mr. Oswald shot and killed the President and then was gunned down on national television, maybe he should be relieved of his Sunday school duties. But he was there. John 3:16. John 3:16.

To this day, I believe in eternal life.

26

GOD'S COUNTRY
by Steven Dietz

Actor Two - 40s - 1983-Present - Various Locations In the U.S. The religious fervor of a madwoman dominates this hallucinatory monologue in which the simple buying of a time capsule is transformed in the woman's troubled mind into a cosmic event reminiscent of the Book of Revelations.

ACTOR TWO: A letter arrives one day. My husband opens it. "The burial of the time capsule will take place in your yard this Sunday. Be prepared to place items of great importance in the capsule, which will be opened after the coming Armageddon, as foretold in the book of Revelations by the prophet John."

Our yard is a mess. There will be cameras and Koppel and my snapdragons won't stand a chance. Women with hair of steel will pummel me with questions and make my dog do tricks he's forgotten. They're trying to make me an event.

My husband begins filling a huge cardboard box with post-apocalyptic belongings. We'll want some magazines, he says. Some playing cards. Beef jerky. I begin to question the value of a Coleman stove in the face of the Four Horsemen and the Seven-Headed Beasts rising up out of the sea. He packs extra socks. I walk out and look at the sky.

Tell us: Why were you chosen and where did the letter come from and what is your religion and do you read our paper and will you sell our breath mints and can you talk with the President and here's another telegram from Israel and Jericho and Idaho and can we get a shot of you with your husband and child and can we get a shot of you cooking and cleaning and breast-feeding and can you sign this for my daughter her name's Edward?

The cardboard box is overflowing with my husband's essentials. Credit cards and condoms and fire insurance are sprouting out of the top. The yard is overflowing with lipstick and technology. My husband puts the box on a dolly and wheels it out through the cheering crowd. I stand in the doorway, holding my baby.

GOD'S COUNTRY

A man in a silk suit, with a huge forehead and ill-fitting teeth, walks through the crowd in my direction. He carries a shiny, stainless steel tube. Three feet long. His forehead is in my face. The cameras are rolling. He is smiling at my baby. The flashes are flashing. He is smiling at my baby. I yell to my husband. He is smiling at my baby. As I tighten my grip, I am holding only myself. Sleeping amid the chaos, my baby is carried away. I see the capsule opened. A prayer is spoken. I see the capsule close around his body. A shaft in the center of the yard is unveiled. The capsule goes in the earth as the reporters go on the air. The crowd explodes into confetti. And I saw an angel come down from heaven. My husband stands in the driveway, wrapping up a movie deal. And the angel laid hold on the Serpent, which is the Devil. My neighbors are giving exclusives. And the Serpent was cast into the bottomless pit and a seal was set upon him that he should deceive the nations no more.

The man with the huge forehead drives away. I grab at the earth. Alpha and Omega. I grab at the air. The first and the last. I stand in my yard. I am holding only myself.

IMAGINING BRAD
by Peter Hedges

Dana Sue Kaye - 30s - Nashville - Present
Brad and his wife have recently moved to Nashville. Urged by
Brad to go to church to meet new friends, his wife attends alone,
only to be confronted by the nosey Dana Sue Kaye, who wants
to know why her husband never appears in public.

DANA: How silly - what is he, a vampire or something? Doesn't
have pictures taken - how strange. And on his wedding day, no less.
What goes on with this guy?
[*Brad's wife is about to speak when:*]
DANA: You must admit that my first impressions are not the kind
one might call impressive...you MUST admit that...
[BRAD'S WIFE: Uhm.]
DANA: Well think about it sweetie...what I know so far...and Dana
Sue Kaye just knows what she has heard...I mean, believe it or not,
I am not all knowing, all powerful...I'm not God...although there is
god in me...I mean, I'm NOT god but I'm part god...and don't ask
what parts are god and what parts aren't because I DON'T
KNOW...I just know that part of me FEELS holy part of the time.
My hair, when I've washed it and blown it dry, sometimes it feels
holy. The white, soft skin on my behind...smooth like a baby's
bottom, unscathed by the sun, unseen by the human eye (except for
Alex, of course)...my littlest toes...how they have been pushed up,
scrunched into the other bigger toes...that part of me has a noble,
almost holy quality. But I'm NOT all knowing and I'm glad I'm not
because THEN I would have to offer advice, I'd have to counsel, I'd
have to solve your problems as well as a billion or more other
people's problems...and frankly I just don't have the time. Time,
my dear, is a thing we're out of. As a planet. I believe this. SO.
What am I saying? I already have my own personal reservations.
About this man of yours. This Brad. This man who you've
committed your entire life and being to...this man who I'm sure you
throw yourself onto nightly, the man who plunges you...who fills

29

you with his juice...this man who does not hesitate to get you on your knees and mount you...this same man just can't seem to make it to church with his beautiful young bride for their first Sunday when they are new in town...(I'd be lying if I said this was acceptable behavior)...one might suppose that he's still sleeping off a very active and passionate night of LOVE making...well, you're here. He isn't. Also, I note that this man refuses to be photographed, even on his wedding day...leaving one to suppose that perhaps his only interest is in photos of the nude kind, the pornographic kind...I mean, I don't know. These are just things a person watching might be left to wonder about. Who is this Brad? What is his story? You know what I'm saying. You know that I'm not criticizing...or judging...you know that...

IMAGINING BRAD
by Peter Hedges

Brad's Wife - 20s - Nashville - Present
Here, Brad's Wife describes her first meeting with Brad. She had been hired to deliver a singing telegram to him, and was shocked to discover that he had no arms or legs.

BRAD'S WIFE: We first met...in Philadelphia...his family comes from...old money...old, <u>old</u> money...I was hired to do a singing telegram...it was my first day on the job and I was taken to this mansion and I thought people live this way?...well, I'd been warned in advance that this was not the uhm typical telegram experience...but I had no idea that what I was singing for was an uh...this little ball of flesh...this bag...this <u>freak</u>...you know...
(The ladies laugh.) so I sang...his parents were there and hundreds of relatives and Brad apparently hadn't uhm been responsive for years...just closed in and bitter...and when I saw him I could see why he had been this way. I tried not to look at him as I sang...but in no time what was at first ugly became soooo beautiful to me...and he must have felt this. Well, my song brought a flood of tears...Brad started talking again right then and there. The family couldn't believe it. And before I knew it they gave me a room in the house...and a nice allowance...and each morning and each evening I would sing for Brad. But it was Brad who proposed. Brad who chose Nashville. He thinks I can make it. He's so supportive. Loves me so much that he would move to this town far away from his family...because of ME...he's so supportive...and I love him.
[DANA: But...]
BRAD'S WIFE: But there are drawbacks, I know...

IS HE STILL DEAD?
by Donald Freed

Nora Joyce - 50s - Zurich - 1941
Nora is the wife of James Joyce, and although she suffers from the pain of arthritis, she remains a woman of great spirit. While in Zurich, she and Joyce visit their daughter, Lucia, who is in a home for the insane. Here, Nora reads a letter from Lucia to Joyce, who is quite ill.

NORA: "Father dear, I am very fond of you. Thanks for the pretty pen. Zurich is not the worst place in the world, is it? Maybe one day you can come with me to the museum, father. I think that you are spending a lot of money on me. Father, if you want to go back to Paris, you would do well to do so. Father dear, I have had too nice a life. I am spoiled. You must both forgive me. I hope that you will come here again. Father, if ever I take a fancy to anybody, I swear to you on the head of Jesus that it will not be because I am not fond of you. Do not forget that. I don't really know what I am writing, Father. At Prangins I saw a number of artists, especially women who seemed to me all very hysterical. Am I to turn out like them? No, it would be better to sell shoes if that can be done with simplicity and truth. And besides, I don't know whether all this I am writing means anything to you.

"I should like to have a life as quiet as I have now, with a garden and perhaps a dog, but nobody is ever contented, isn't that so? So many people were envious of me and of Mama because you are too good. It is a pity that you don't like Ireland, for after all, it is a lovely country, if I may judge by the pictures I have seen, and the stories I have heard. Who knows what fate has in store for us? At any rate, in spite of the fact that life seems full of light this evening, here, if ever I should go away, it would be to a country which belongs in a way to you, isn't that true, Father? I am still writing silly things, you see. I send you both affectionate greetings, and I hope that you did not miss your train the other day. --Lucia"

IS HE STILL DEAD?
by Donald Freed

Nora Joyce - 50s - Zurich - 1941
Joyce is near death and misses the joys of eating and drinking.
The stalwart Nora stays by his side and fantasizes to him about
better times ahead.

NORA: Shhh, give over, Jim, listen to me, now: You'll be right
as rain back in Zurich. Walkin' with Giorgio--you'll be a new man
and so will he. You won't touch a drop, and you'll both be
yourselves again--for the boy's sake, for peace's sake. You'll land
on your feet, there. You'll take the air, and I'll cook for yez. All
your favorites--tripe and onions with white sauce; roast chicken
stuffed with mashed potatoes, hmmm...
[*(Joyce breathes regularly, now, still clutching her hand. There is
an occasional word or sound from him.)*]
NORA: *(Continuing)* Shh...Sure, it's I'll help with your proofs,
again. And Mrs. Weaver, she'll get the royalty money through to
us, somehow, no need to worry...Shh--and I'll cook hot grocers'
peas for yez, and even corned beef, and colcannon with butter and
onions and kale and turnips like Annie Barnacle did, and boiled eggs
and rashers with slices of tomatoes--the way you used to wolf it
down...*(She sings again.)* "Though the way be weary..."--Soft days,
and then we'll have Lucia with us again; sure, this war'll be over in
no time, and we'll have her back--sure, God shuts one door and
opens another...*(Resisting her own grief) (Continuing)* Shh...And
chops of lamb and pork...We'll have her back, like she was,
before...And for your birthday, leg of lamb with fresh peas and
parsnips and...*(She breaks for a moment)*...turnips...Christmas
breakfast--bacon and eggs and blood sausage--and then a goose at
four o'clock and a Limerick ham...And we'll all sing the old songs
around the piano, and we'll dance, too--you'll see. And they'll
come from all over the world to call on us. All the little fellahs like
Hemingway and Gide and Proust--no, he's dead--
[*(Joyce mumbles something in his sleep about Rahoon.)*]

33

IS HE STILL DEAD?

NORA: *(Continuing)* "Rahoon" is it? Sure, I know it by heart:
"Rain on Rahoon falls softly, softly falling,
Where my dark lover lies.
Sad is his voice that calls me, sadly calling
At grey moonrise..."
Sure, aren't they all buried there? Annie Barnacle and me poor
dumb Da, too, and Michael Bodkin, that poor boy that loved me and
that you've been jealous of, for nothin', all these years--because you
were my first and only one, Jim, and that's the Gospel alls of
it... *(Nora waits a moment until he seems to drop off. A warning
siren in the distance. Nora goes to the telephone and whispers into
it.)* S'il-vous-plait, le porter pour les..oui, send the man up for the
luggage, tout de suite--comprenez-vous?--oui, merci, tout de suite...

KURU
by Josh C. Manheimer

Mary Lou - 30s - New Guinea - 1950s
Mary Lou Anderson has followed her fiance, Dr. Arthur
Roman, into the heart of the cannibal-infested jungles of Paupau
New Guinea. This plucky farm girl from the midwest isn't in
the least intimidated by her new surroundings. Indeed, she feels
a calling to help the people of the village that they inhabit by
teaching cooking classes. Here she instructs the native women
on the best way to make a Thanksgiving turkey.

MARY LOU: *(Tying an apron around herself)* Okay, ladies. Quiet
down now. Yes, let's begin. Now I understand Arthur...Dr.
Roman has taught you all a little English so try and stick with me.
Tonight we're going to prepare a fun, easy Holiday recipe you and
your family will cherish. I tell the girls back home, cooking is more
than refilling the old trough. Sure, if you want your kids to drive
semis for the rest of their lives, just blindly go ahead, smear the
same old whatever on a loaf of Wonder Bread. But if you want to
make a difference in their lives, if you want to Influence World
Events, now take notes here. It takes, yes, courage. Moral fiber.
You see, and we are all guilty, we take the easy way, we neglect
ourselves, we leave the curlers in, trudge into the kitchen and just
throw together whatever. But this is where we must catch ourselves
and ask, "Is this bologna sandwich really a courageous act?" Or in
your case is this--what?--this Python grinder, just another example
of our own, you know, lack of control over our lives. Because one
day you'll wake up and find yourself, alone in your hut in all your
nakedness. Staring at the same old pie tins asking is this all there is
to life? Are we really such criminals if we take a risk and serve,
say, Thanksgiving turkey without stuffing and brown gravy? And
this is my point. Who but us is going to change the rules?
Certainly not them. Men. Uh! No. It is our duty to ask ourselves,
what are others around the world serving for supper? Not your
friends next door. But far away. For me, I have to say, as repulsed

as I am, by the idea of Termite Stew, maybe, just maybe, I have to accept the fact it is a tasty treat I may want to serve to my ladies back home. And you...when I show you tonight how to whip together Little Cocktail Party Frankfurters, you must be brave. You must say, if there is going to be peace in the world, if I am going to accept other culture, to see through other people's eyes, I must first acknowledge there are other Tastes. We must meet halfway at the table. I know this may be hard to swallow. You may think I am a no-good radical. You may look at me askance. Your husbands may beat you with a branch for changing the menu, but if Progress is to be made, this is as it must be.

KURU
by Josh C. Manheimer

Mary Lou - 30s - New Guinea - 1950s
When Mary Lou inadvertently stumbles onto the cure for the dreaded disease, Kuru, Arthur begs her to leave the jungle and return to Iowa. He has spent years trying to discover the cure and is humiliated that Mary Lou has found it so easily. She tells him firmly that she intends to stay in New Guinea.

MARY LOU: I called you to apologize. Not to be argued with. When I passed out, I dreamed I saw finally what my mission is here on this good earth. I dreamed I saw myself standing on a hill cooking for the world. I was feeding everyone. And I started sending out Chinese food to the French and French food to poor people in Brazil. I cooked pot roast for the Palestinians and grapefruit salad for the Greeks. I taught the Dali Lama how to bake a potato knish and the Pope how to whip up a chocolate shake. The students were coming in like crazy. I was teaching, Arthur. I was teaching the world humility. I had everyone waking up and eating differently. Finally looking down at their plates and saying, Hey, this is good! I was making people WAKE UP and realize we are all humans. How can we judge? How can we begin to judge another. Unless we can sit down and taste with another man's tongue, taste what they have suffered, taste what they believe, taste where they hurt, taste what they love, how can we ever begin to Judge? And the world saw. For the first time. I've been given a gift, Arthur. A power. It is my calling. I'm sorry. I cannot return. These are my people now. This is my place. You'll just have to explain.
[DR. ROMAN: But, Mary Lou. You can save souls in Iowa.]
MARY LOU: Iowa will survive without me. These poor folks will all die dead unless they learn how to eat right. The women have to get control of the kitchen again. The men have screwed it just like they always do. We'll start slow. But we'll get 'em to finally shut up and eat what's in front of 'em. That's all I ask. Just shut up for two seconds and eat what we women put in front of you.

37

LETTICE & LOVAGE
by Peter Shaffer

Lettice Douffet - 40s-50s - England - Present

Lettice Douffet is a highly imaginative and romantic woman with a flair for the dramatic. She exploits these qualities daily in her job as tour guide at Fustian House, a sixteenth century English manor house. To relieve the monotony, Lettice embellishes her speeches to the tour groups with her own exciting interpretations of an otherwise dull family history.

LETTICE: You are looking at what is indisputably the most famous staircase in England!...The *Staircase of Ennoblement!* On the night of February the second, 1585--a brilliant snowy night--John Fustian laid before his sovereign here in this hall a monumental feast! The tables were piled high with hedgehogs, puffins, and coneys!--and a hundred of the liveliest courtiers stood salivating to consume it! *(Increasingly excited by her tale)* Suddenly she appeared--Gloriana herself, the Virgin Queen of England!--encrusted from bosom to ankle with a blaze of diamonds presented to her by the Czar Ivan the Terrible, who had seen a portrait of her in miniature and lost a little of his icy heart to her chaste looks! Smiling, she set foot upon the first stair, up there! Alas, as she did so--at that precise moment--she slipped and would have plunged headlong down all fifteen polished and bruising steps, had not her host--standing precisely where I stand now, *at the very bottom--leapt in a single bound* the whole height of the staircase to where she stood and saved her! *(One or two gasp with amazement.)* Imagine the scene! Time as if suspended! A hundred beribboned guests frozen like Renaissance statues, arms outstretched in powerless gesture! Eyes wide with terror in the flare of torches!...And then suddenly John Fustian moves! He who up to that moment has lived his whole life as a dull turgid yeoman, breaks the spell! Springs forward--upward--rises like a bird--like feathered Mercury--*soars* in one astounding leap the whole height of these stairs, and at the last possible moment catches her in his loyal arms, raises her high above his head, and rose-cheeked with triumph cries up to her: "Adored Majesty! Adored and *En*dored Majesty! Fear not! You are safe--And your hedgehogs await!"

LETTICE & LOVAGE
by Peter Shaffer

Lettice Douffet - 40s-50s - England - Present
Here, Lettice conducts yet another rousing tour through the
musty old manor house.

LETTICE: The incident I have just described to you--in which the
Virgin Queen Elizabeth was saved from almost certain death by a
feat of daring completely unachievable today *by even the greatest
Olympic athlete*--is only one of many deeds of high drama which
have been enacted upon the stage of this historic staircase. *(Pause.)*
Not all of them, alas, were so happy in their outcome. The ensuing
century was in every way darker, and the doings on its staircases
were correspondingly more murky...It was upon these very stairs
one hundred years later, that the most *terrible* of all events connected
with this house occurred--on Mid-summer morning, sixteen hundred
and eighty-nine. *(All look expectant. Lettice warms to her tale.)*
This day was intended to celebrate the marriage of Miss Arabella
Fustian to the handsomest young lordling in the region. The bride
was a radiantly beautiful girl of eighteen--"the catch of the Country,"
as she was called. On the morning of her wedding her father, Sir
Nicholas, stood exactly where I stand now--waiting to escort his only
daughter to the church. The door of the bedchamber opened above
(She points; all look eagerly.) and out stepped this exquisite creature
in a miasma of white samite. It is not hard to imagine her father
staring up at her, tears welling in his old eyes--she about to descend
these stairs for the last time a maiden! And then--ah, suddenly! a
terrible drumming is heard! A frantic pounding along the oak
gallery--and toward her, galloping at full speed, is Charger, the
faithful wolf-hound of the family, wild with excitement at smelling
the nuptial baked meats roasting in the kitchen below! In his
hurtling frenzy he knocks the girl aside! She staggers--flails the air--
shoots out her hand for the banister, which alas is too far from her,
and *falls headlong* after the beast!...her lovely body rolling like a
cloud down the fifteen stairs you see, until at last with one appalling

jolt it comes to rest at her father's feet!... *(She points to the spot, at her own.)* No Mercury he, but ancient and arthritic, he stoops to touch her. Is she dead? No, the Saints be praised! Her neck is unbroken. *(A pause.)* In a dreadful echo of the gesture with which his ancestor won the family title, he catches the girl up in his arms and, watched by the agonized dog, carries her upward to her room. A room she was never to leave again.   Arabella regained consciousness, yes, but her legs, which had danced the Gavotte and the Scotch Jig as no legs had ever danced them, were now twisted beneath her in mockery of the love-knots which grace the plaster ceiling above you!   *(All look up.)*   By her own choice the girl immured herself in that chamber up there for life, receiving no visitors but howling incessantly the Marriage Hymn which had been specially composed for her by Henry Purcell himself!...The Family Chronicle records that her attendants were likewise distorted.   I quote it for you. "The wretched lady would employ as domestics only those who were deformed in the legs and haunches: knotted women, bunchbacks, swivel-hips, and such as had warpage and osseous misalignment of the limbs." Servants of all shapes clawed their way daily up this staircase, which was now known no longer as the Staircase of Aggrandizement, but the *Staircase of Wound and Woe!* This name it has retained ever since.

THE MAGIC ACT
by Laurence Klavan

Mona Kale - 30s - Massachusetts Courtroom and Mind and Memory of Mona Kale - Present

Mona is a woman accused of murdering a young couple. Their happiness had evidently made Mona quite bitter about her own loneliness. Mona addresses the jury and declares her innocence. She explains that she is a victim of a nation addicted to sensationalism.

MONA: Ladies and gentlemen of the Jury...I'm innocent, innocent, I tell you! I didn't kill them! *(Beat.)* But no one will believe me. All they care about are the headlines, is the sensationalism. *(She picks up a stack of newspapers, starts rifling through them.)* "Lonely Gal Murders Couple in Love"..."High School Sweethearts Slain by Bitter Spinster"..."Unmarried Vulture Butchers Married Lovebirds." *(She flings them down again.)* You know, when you're little, you think you might grow up and stand for something someday. But you never imagine you'll become the national symbol for the lonely and the insane. It's like becoming famous for the one thing you're most ashamed of. "Biggest Goiter in the United States." "Least Educated Man in the World." So sometimes strangers in the street look down and find the I'm holding their hand. So maybe I rent so many movies I've earned a "Frequent Fantasizer" discount at my video store. Who's really so different from me? *That's* the question that Brad and Judy and Chuck and Sue avoid before they go to the weather. Alan and Annabelle *were* different-- *that's* what killed them and *that's* what they're afraid to say. They were blessed by something--something unearthly, something fantastic. And all I could ever do was stand there and reach out and touch them as they passed and hope some of them would come off in my hand. *(Turns to dead bodies.)* I didn't slap the kisses from their lips, I didn't stop their hearts! *(Turns back.)* But you have to believe in magic to believe that, and it's easier to believe in murder. The media can do their prime-time specials, but that's just realism, that's just TV. When *I* remember Alan and Annabelle, it's like a flashback in a film. Everything goes all fuzzy, like Vaseline is being spread on my eyes. But it's the truth, so it'll never make the news. See, Alan and Annabelle... *(Lights slowly shift.)* I met them when we were all just kids, in a suburb near New York. It's really only twenty miles from here, but now it seems like a continent away, like America is to Russia, like I'd have to be smuggled across a border to reach a place that innocent again. It was called Gentle Gushing, Long Island, and I lived on Pistachio Nut Lane. *(Exaggeratedly pleasant music starts. Lights hit L. and R. The dead bodies exit. Alan, a dark, reasonably attractive teenager, enter S.R. Annabelle, a light, reasonably attractive teenager, enters L.)* Alan lived on one side of town, the child of comedians, in a house where everything was gay. *(The shadow of his Father is seen tap-dancing near Alan.)* Anna lived on the other side, the daughter of a miserable mother and a soon-to-be-dead father who owned a chain of for-profit prisons. It was a home where everything was sad. *(The shadow of her Mother is seen beating her breast and slapping her own face near Anna.)* They would meet in the middle, in the place between the idiotic and the awful, the horrible and the moronic.

MAIDS OF HONOR
by Joan Casademont

Izzy - 20s - Marblehead, MA - Present
Izzy and Annie want to stop their sister, Monica, from marrying
a man they know is a crook. Izzy, a fledgling reporter, here
describes to a fellow journalist who has written the expose on
Monica's fiance, an event from her life as a runaway model.

IZZY: See, I'd always hated how I felt when I had to walk or skip
or jump down some goddamn runway to some ditzy music to please
some son-of-a-bitch. This one time, see, at this big fall showing in
Boston, I was wearing this ridiculous mink and halfway down the
runway I got this idea--like a lightning bolt in my brain--that I
should just rip it off and dance the way I wanted! Well, I ripped off
the coat and threw it and before I know it I'd ripped off the dress
underneath and the underwear too! I was naked except for these
heels, so I kicked those off and started to jump up and down on all
fours, like a gorilla! I spotted this big fruit basket and I just started
to gorge, I was spitting out cherry pits, peach pits, plum pits, you
name it, I spit it! God, I was having such a good time! Well the
music went screeching off, people ran, and the designer started
screaming in my ear, "YOU FREAK! YOU ANIMAL! YOU
FREAK!" when the security guards hauled me away. I just
screamed back, "I AM A HUMAN BEING, DESCENDED FROM
APES! DESCENDED FROM APES!"...Time to quit the biz,
eh?..You wanna go get a drink and figure out how to proceed with
the damn story?

MAIDS OF HONOR
by Joan Casademont

Monica - 30s - Marblehead, MA - Present
Monica, a successful television talk show host, defends her
bitchiness to Annie by pointing out that she has managed to
survive in the very competitive world of TV.

MONICA: I am sorry I'm such a bitch! You know, it helps
though, being a bitch sometimes. I mean, I wouldn't have gotten my
own talk show if I wasn't a bitch. Besides, it would make me very
happy to just once hear someone--i.e., a man--define "bitch". I ask
my producer, my cameramen, my male staff members all the time
to just give me real honest to God definition and they can't! They
say, "A bitch is a bitch. You just know a bitch when you see one."
Well, I don't accept that! They can't define it because what bitch
really means is a driven and in command woman. My producer
comes into that studio like a wild bull 'cause somebody fucked up,
and everybody goes, "Whoa, look at that Ralph, what a man!, some
day he's gonna run the network." I come into that studio with a
faint trace of smoke comin' outta one nostril 'cause one of my staff
flat out gave me the wrong info and everybody goes, "Whoa, look
out, the bitch is raggin' out again!" I tell you, Annie, it is a
battlefield out there, we're all wearing Armani but the sexes are
simply not from the same planet and together we have a national
epidemic of total misunderstanding. *(She sighs, exhausted.)*
Still, I'm sorry if to you I acted like a--well, like a bitch.

MARY AND LIZZIE
by Frank McGuinness

Queen Victoria - 30s - Any Place - Any Time
Mary and Lizzie Burns wander the earth, meeting people and discussing ideas. Here they encounter a young Queen Victoria, who offers a surprisingly insightful rumination on the future of her country.

VICTORIA: I'm born to rule. My destiny, England's destiny, decreed by God, by fate and by me. A myth I am, but not yet a monster. There will be wonderful stories about my terrible life. As a child, they dressed me in black. It was in preparation. Not for being queen, but for being a woman. ˙What is England life? Go and find out. I can tell you one thing. It isn't content. So it roams the world, looking for contentment. And finds it nowhere. For no one wants it. That's a secret between me and the empire. Put it under your hat, when you can afford one. I worry for poor England when the wandering's over. Where will it go then but into itself, and what will it find? A tenement. The England that was wont to conquer others now makes a conquest of itself. Some third-rate isle lost among her seas. How shall we cope? By lying, I suppose. Methinks I am a prophet newly blessed. The old order changeth, yielding place to the new. Find it. Find it in Manchester. Would you excuse me? I must rule. I have an empire to govern. May as well enjoy it while it lasts. I send best wishes to your kingdom under the sea. We must exchange ambassadors. I'll speak to Lord Melbourne. *(Moves to exit.)* Forgive me.

MARY AND LIZZIE
by Frank McGuinness

Jenny - 30s - Any Place - Any Time
Mary, Lizzie and Engles are entertained by Karl and Jenny
Marx. Jenny serves her guests fresh strawberries and then
confronts them all with what displeases her about her husband
and his economic theories.

JENNY: Offer our guests food, husband. I apologize for the
poverty of the fare, but the dish is beautiful. I like to look at it. It
convinces me I am a wealthy woman. *(They each take a strawberry
and eat.)* As a young woman, I was quite pretty. Do eat more
strawberries, they're quite delicious. Forgive my nerves. I bought
the strawberries all by myself. Are you proud of me, Karl? Karl
has lived with my nerves so long he scarcely notices them. I drive
him out of the house. He is a good man, I've made him what he is
today. We love each other. For him I would pawn my life. Which
is just as well. It is the only thing we have not pawned yet.
(Laughs.) My strength is I find it all so funny. Karl Marx cannot
feed his family; his wife and mainstay cannot help her husband.
Aren't we silly-billies? I do encourage him now with the odd
extravagant gesture. That is why I burned the money. Have you
ever watched money burning? A piece of paper, turning to ash. I
was conducting a scientific experiment. Will it burn to gold? It
didn't, Karl. Ash to ash and dust to dust, money is death, my love,
and you have been dealing in death for so long, my darling, I have
lost direction and you are losing control, for the house is falling
about our ears and now I only hear you speak to me in the
crumbling walls and squeaking doors and the holes in the roof and
your bloody books. I would like to put a match to your books and
watch them blaze like an old boot and say, this is my life and if life
be a wheel, I am spinning out of control. You cannot help me,
husband. Help me. Help me. I am a noble woman. I am wife to
Karl Marx, who cannot feed his family but who would feed all
mankind. It's a conspiracy against me. You and your whores, Mr.

MARY AND LIZZIE

Engels, conspire with the world against me. I do realize what is going on around me. *(Silence.)* Eat. Eat the strawberries. I picked them myself. *(Jenny squeezes strawberries in her hands until they are red.)* When I was young and could look in the mirror, I once saw myself like a tree, and then one night I lit a candle and Karl appeared. I got such a shock. I thought it was my husband, he took my breath away. Perhaps he didn't. We've travelled together through life. To where, I don't know. Do eat these strawberries. To death, I suppose. I picked them myself. *(Looks at her hands.)* I have a mind of my own. Fetch me the tray, Karl. *(Marx goes to her with the tray. Jenny takes the sheets of paper and wipes her hands with them.)* Read my hands. What's written on the paper. Handwriting. Only I can read your handwriting. Shall I whisper a sinister prophecy of coming catastrophe? *(Jenny whispers, reading from the crumpled paper.)* All fixed, fast-frozen relations with their train of ancient and venerable prejudices and opinions are swept away, all new-formed ones become antiquated before they can ossify. All that is solid melts into air, all that is holy is profaned, and man is at last compelled to face with sober senses his real contradictions of life and his relations with his kind. *(Silence.)* Well, are you proud of your wife? Did you believe she'd think that up? I wrote that, not you, my love. Isn't this my handwriting? *(Marx turns from her.)* Solid, melting into air, my husband. Holy, now profaned, our life. His sober senses recoil from me. Face me, face your kind. Am I your contradiction? Are we not speaking? My husband and I are in opposition tonight. I am afraid he will brand me revolutionary. Well, it is high time revolutionaries should openly, in the face of the whole world, publish their views, their aims, their tendencies, and meet this nursery tale--

MIRIAM'S FLOWERS
by Migdalia Cruz

Delfina - 30s - New York City - Present
Nando and Delfina mourn the death of their young son, Puli.
As Delfina packs up Puli's clothes for the church, Nando sleeps
close by. The grief-stricken Delfina speaks softly to the sleeping
Nando of the sneakers that Puli had wanted so badly, and of the
clothes that he had been dressed in for his funeral.

DELFINA: He only wore his suit once before...To Pepe's wedding.
I said it was stupid to buy a suit. Kids in suits look like midgets,
especially boys. Or like monkeys. They always put monkeys in
suits for T.V. shows. I didn't want my boy to dress like a monkey,
but the bride wanted it like that--real formal. -- The shirt I had to
borrow because the shirt he had didn't have no buttons and you
know, I couldn't find no buttons in the house to fix it, so a lady
from the church gave me her son's old shirt, but it didn't even look
old. It looked new. I think her son, Cholo, was always too fat for
it. So Puli got it. The bowtie I got for him to wear on the first day
of school. He wanted to wear a t-shirt though, so he put his bowtie
on the belt loop of his pants. He wore that almost all the time.
When he fell asleep with all his clothes on, I could wake him up by
unclipping that tie--he'd shoot up like an arrow, pull it out of my
hands and go back to sleep with that tie safe under his pillow...The
socks are Miree's. All his socks had holes, and even though we had
to fold them over twice, I think it's better, socks without holes.
Especially since the shoes are new. He wanted those shoes for a
long time--white, Converse All-Star Hi-Tops.
     Everybody said sneakers are disrespectful, but who was
wearing them? Puli, and he knew what he wanted. I made Miree
go to the church and ask for money. She hates me now. But Puli
got his sneakers. They looked good on him, I bet. I--I couldn't
look. Or maybe when I looked I just couldn't see...They did a good
job on his face. They had to build his head up again because mostly
it--a good job is what everybody told me. Miree put a rose on top

of him before they closed him up. That's supposed to only be for women, but you can't tell Miree what to do about nothing.--I wish--I wish they had just showed his face. I didn't like seeing his arm like that, it gave Miree nightmares. She's not strong, like me.

MIRIAM'S FLOWERS
by Migdalia Cruz

Miriam - 16 - New York City - Present

Sixteen year-old Miriam is perhaps the most affected by Puli's death. She misses her little brother in ways that she cannot put into words. Inability to express her grief has helped to start a horrifying ritual of self-mutilation, but even as she cuts herself with a razor, she is still unable to feel pain. In church, she confronts a statue of Christ, and questions him about his own wounds.

MIRIAM: I'm the invisible girl, Mary...always searching for a hole in the wall to pull myself through to get to the other side. The other side is only for me, I could see myself then. I could feel my fingertips then and the pointy pieces of skin being torn down the sides of my fingers. I could see the scars then, on the bottom of my thumbs from the Wilkinson Swords--I write on myself with them. I carve myself in to my hands. And for Lent, Mary, I'll cover them with purple cloth. I keep my gloves on in the church, until everybody leaves and then I come to you. To show you. *(She takes off her gloves.)* See? I show you mine and then I can touch your... *(She places her hands on the carved wounds of Jesus.)* They feel so fresh Jesus. Like mine. I can smell the blood on them. Smells like violets and sweet coffee with five sugars--Like Ma takes it... *(Pause.)* I'm never gonna die--not from my wounds anyway. I never go in deep and I don't make them long. I make little points that add up to a picture, a flower picture. And sometimes they so pretty they make me cry, and I like that, because when I get those tears on my hands and on my arms, they sting, and then I know I'm alive cause it hurts so bad. Does that happen to you too?

MORE FUN THAN BOWLING
by Steven Dietz

Molly - 16 - Midwest - Present
Jake is the owner of the Dust Bowl Bowling Alley. In his life
he has known the love of four women: three wives and one
daughter, Molly. Here, Molly describes her parents' first
meeting and courtship.

MOLLY: Works like a charm. *(Goes to her bike and unlocks the
chain and wraps it up during the following.)* My mom's name is
Maggie. Wife number one. Very beautiful. Very rich. She met
Dad when he was on his way to the Wyoming Conservatory of
Music. Their eyes met in the train station. She going northeast, he
southwest. They held their gaze as their trains departed--leaving
them standing on opposite platforms. She in her silk dress and high
heels, he in his overalls and feed cap. She liked his style. They
went in a bar with an adjacent bowling alley. These were the days
of pin setters--young kids who set the pins by hand after each ball.
Two hours later they were run out of that alley because my dad
threw a bowling ball so hard and sprayed pins so far that none of
those boys would stand back there and set 'em. She liked his style.
Dad bought his first pair of dark socks and the marriage was held in
New York City. They acquired a house and a car and a business
with Maggie's money. She threw a lot of parties. Dad bought his
first necktie and worked a twenty-hour week behind a desk, and
made more in one month than this daddy had made on the farm in
one year. They had a daughter and named her Molly and when she
was ten, Dad found a new bicycle in the front hall with an envelope
taped to the handlebars. Inside the envelope was five thousand
dollars and my birth certificate. Maggie was gone. Dad bought this
piece of land which included the only bowling alley in town. He
worked the counter and I set the pins till we got automated. Then
I worked the counter with Lois, who was wife number two till she
died. Then I worked the counter with Loretta, who was wife
number three till she died. Now, I work the counter alone and Dad
tries not to get married.

51

MORE FUN THAN BOWLING
by Steven Dietz

Lois - 20s-30s - Midwest - Present
Lois was Jake's second wife. Although she never shared his
passion for bowling, she did share his love of life. Here, she
tells a tale of a night in her youth that she attended a dance at
the VFW to her best friend, Loretta, who was to eventually
become wife number three.

LOIS: About ten years ago. We went to a dance at the V.F.W. hall
on the Fourth of July. All the guys came dressed as their favorite
president. Half came as Washington. Half as Lincoln. Vo-Tech's
not long in the history department. My date came as F.D.R. so he
wouldn't have to dance. *(Pause.)* We sat for hours in the corner,
eating mints. Then he asked if I'd ever seen a "real...smooth...
pickup." And I said maybe not, and he lifted me up over his head
and took me out to the parking lot. That was pretty smooth, I said
and he said "That wasn't it. This is it." He pointed to his shiny
silver Ford pickup truck with metallic green shell on back. "Want
to get inside and get to know each other?" he said. Before I knew
it, someone had sucked out all my common sense with a straw and
I said "Sure" and we sat there smelling the fresh vinyl seat covers.
He didn't say a word. I turned on the radio. He turned it off. He
said he had something to show me and he unzipped his pants and
reached way down in them and pulled our a very...small...key.
"This key opens my gun rack" and sure enough there was his twelve
gauge shotgun locked to a rack behind our heads and he took down
that gun and began to clean it with his white handkerchief. He
explained every detail of that gun to me during the next hour as he
caressed it with that handkerchief. Then he loaded it. Then he
lifted the edge of my skirt with it and said "Now, what are *you*
gonna show *me. (Pause.)*
[LORETTA: *(Impatient.)* Okay, okay. So, what did you do?]
LOIS: *(Pause.)* After showing him the entire contents of my
purse..only four minutes had elapsed. So, I started to unbutton

52

my blouse. And he started to smile. Then I stopped. I said "For the good stuff we need to get in the back." "Under the shell?" he said. "Yeah," I said. "I just put new carpeting back there" he said. "Your choice," I said, and after considering it for a moment...he nodded. "Take off all your clothes," I said. "Even my shorts?" he said. "Especially your shorts," I said. So there he was, naked in the back of the shell. And there I was, about to climb in--when I grabbed his clothes, slammed the cover shut, locked him in and drove the pickup to the front door of the V.F.W. Hall. *(Stands.)* I walked inside, grabbed the microphone from the stage and yelled "HEY, I GOT A KEG OF BEER IN THE BACK OF MY PICKUP. EVERYBODY HELP THEMSELVES." That metallic shell didn't last long, and F.D.R. would've been proud of how fast that boy ran away naked into the night.

QUEEN OF THE LEAKY ROOF CIRCUIT
by Jimmy Breslin

Juliet Queen Booker - 45 - New York - Present
Juliet Queen Booker is a 45 year-old black woman who has just
been notified by the City Marshall that she is being evicted from
her Brooklyn apartment. Here she gives a moving and graphic
account of life in one of New York's welfare hotels. Indeed,
she would rather die than be forced to move.

JULIET: A welfare hotel is thirty months of living with crack
smokers. Crack! You really ought to see it. A white chunk only
as big as your thumbnail. You buy it in a little plastic vial, the kind
they have filled with sequins for ladies to buy. Cost ten dollar.
They put it in a glass pipe and smoke it. Because it keeps goin' out,
you got to keep relighting it. That's why you always see them usin'
lighters. Chunk of crack only lasts ten minutes, but there must be
no high like it. Whoever invented crack is the genius of the drug
business. Heroin, cocaine, they doan mean nothin'. The crack will
not go away. It is here for as long as there's people to breathe it in.
They take one, they go crazy, and they need another one right away.
They drop these empty vials on the floor, you understand, and all the
little children be combin' the floor for the vials. They get a whole
garbage bag full of vials, take them to the pusher and he be givin'
them all free crack for returning the vials. Free crack to ten year
old. Ask anybody. Crack is the worst thing ever to happen to poor
people. Because it is never goin' away. Never. People like it too
much and there isn't much to like down here. *(As she talks, the
lighters come closer and she stands and shakes her finger at the
lighters. The lighters fade away.)*
   *(Juliet holds up a box of cereal and a small pint container
of milk.)* When the milk be gone, you borrow another dollar and get
some more. We be goin' four, five straight days with cereal for
every meal. You got no stoves in a welfare hotel. You got 700 hot
plates in this hotel. People got hot plates on top of cardboard,
newspapers. So this isn't really a hotel I'm livin' in. It's a furnace

54

that hasn't happened to start up yet. *(She holds up the cereal box.)* Even eatin' with no stove doan mean you be safe. Some crackhead start a fire anyway. T' other day, two little babies be burned up in the hallway. The mother be lookin' for them in the smoke. Then she sees this fire through the smoke. Her babies burnin' live right in front of her eyes.

You stay in a welfare hotel like this for eighteen months. Then...maybe...they find me an apartment. The first one the welfare took me to, the door had no locks and the apartment next door was empty account of a fire and they all be standing inside smoking crack. Second apartment had rats run all around when we walk in. Skinny woman next door be selling crack right out of her door. I say to my little Cynthia, "child, don't you look around. I don't want you to remember bein' here." The social worker say the rules are, I be seein' one more apartment, and if I don' take it, I be goin' to the bottom of the ladder, right to the shelter and start all over again. The third and last apartment she brought me to was right here. I see the roof leakin', I doan care, I kiss the floor right here. I tell you I'd as soon die as get thrown out.

QUEEN OF THE LEAKY ROOF CIRCUIT
by Jimmy Breslin

Beatrice Jackson - 30-50 - New York - Present
Beatrice Jackson is Juliet's closest friend and staunch supporter
in her unflagging effort to fight the city's eviction notice.
Beatrice herself has not been left untouched by bureaucracy's
sting as she details here in a frightening story of being raped by
her husband.

BEATRICE: Now Juliet be out lookin' for a piece of court paper.
That's when my trouble started. Piece of court paper. *(Beatrice
now starts to go through her purse, talking to herself. She takes out
a piece of folded legal paper, looks at it and is affected by it.)* Look
at this all chewed up. Just what happened to it, too. Chewed up.
This be a court order of protection. You get it when somebody like
your husband beats you up. If he come to the house all you do is
get the police and show this paper to them and they take the man out
of your house. This be a paper to protect my body. Huh. That is
all you get. A piece of paper. Let me tell you about my order of
protection. I got it on my first husband Robert. He got up from bed
one night and comes back four years later. Leaves me with his kids
and no money. All of a sudden, here he is, walks back in, gets into
bed. Gets up, disappears two, three days, then just comes back in.
I told him to go away from my apartment. To leave my apartment
and to leave me alone. And I packed his things up to tell him to
take it with him. Man beat me. The police write up the complaint
and leave. Nothing ever happened. I throwed him out. He come
back right through there. *(Pointing to window.)* I don't mean
exactly in here. I got the very same window in my house right
downstairs here. My husband come by, through my fire escape in
the apartment. He had a gun. It was a silver gun and he hit me in
my head or anywhere he could reach. He hit me in the head and
busted my head. When I woke up there were medics and the police
were there and my husband Robert be gone. They say, "We walk
him around the block, cool him down. It's better than y'all havin'

him arrested. You don't want to do that, do you?" I said, I want him arrested. I go to court and they give me this paper. *(She holds it up.)* I believed it was good. DA give it to me. Said you just keep that and show it. It be an order of protection. He can't come near you. If he does, call the police and show them the order. DA say he keep in contact with me. Bullshit! *(Holds up the order of protection.)* Man be givin' me this paper, it meant nothin'. One night I went to a store and when I come home, the door was cracked open a little and I opened it and he put a knife in my neck. I reached slow into my pocketbook and I take out the paper the DA gave me and he say to me, "You put that paper in your mouth." Jabs my neck harder with his knife. I put the order of protection in my mouth and I chew it and he say he stab me dead right there if I didn't take my clothes off. I told him that the kids were there. He told me he'd stab me through the neck if I didn't take my clothes off. I did. He took off his pants and had sex with me. Court order in my mouth. My husband raped me and my kids watched from the doorway. Court order in my mouth. When he left, I took the court order out of my mouth, all chewed up, put it back in my pocketbook. That's what a court order done for me. *(She sighs and puts away the paper.)*

SANTIAGO
by Manuel Pereiras [García]

Pilar - 38 - Santiago - Present
Pilar is a simple laundress with social aspirations. Here she describes the disappointment that she felt when she finally married her wealthy lover and discovered that due to the government takeover, "high society" was no more.

PILAR: Mamino married me--Now that I'm a grandmother. Did you know that? Did you know I had an older daughter? She doesn't call me mother or anything but she respects me now. She sends me pictures. I didn't raise her. You know who raised her? Mamino's wife. There are things that never get to be what they're supposed to be. Now I'm married to him but it's not the same. I always wanted to be his wife and go to the club. Now I'm married to him but it's not the same. The rich are gone and the club is not the same. I'm his wife but the rich are not longer there. So when he took me there it wasn't like going to the club. When I crossed the doors on Mamino's arm, it was not the same place. I felt so bad. The night before the takeover I was there. My brother is a bongo player and he got me in. I was there that night. They knew it was going to happen. The rich knew there was going to be a takeover. They threw a party. A ball. Everyone dressed--long dress and all. The mayor, the ex lady mayor, was wearing a white dress with thin shoulder straps. If she saw me in the streets she always said hello but at the club she didn't.
[SHE: High society is hypocritical--that's what's so appealing about them.]
PILAR: Toward the end of the evening she wiped her forehead. She dropped her handkerchief; she noticed it; she looked at it and decided not to pick it up. I saw it. The next morning was the takeover. The doors of the club were opened to the people. I was among the first. I went to look for the handkerchief. That's why I went. The people went wild and started looting. I found the handkerchief and took it. I knew where it was. Her initial was

embroidered on it. "V." It was not a fine handkerchief. It was simple: one of those handkerchiefs embroidered by girls in third grade in private schools as the nuns guided their white fingers smiling softly and nodding. I had always wanted one. Ever since the days I used to go help my mother clean the floor in their schools. I guess I could have bought one later but it wouldn't have been the same. I used to have it with me all the time even if my name doesn't start with a "V." But I misplaced it. I don't know where it is. Perhaps it got in someone's laundry and I'll never see it again.

SARA
by Gotthold Ephraim Lessing
translated by Ernest Bell

Sara - 20s - England - 1755
Sara, a young woman of virtue, has run away with her rakish lover Mellefont. Tortured by guilt Sara is plagued with nightmares in which accusing voices remind her of her lost chastity. When she confronts Mellefont with her fears for their future he attempts to placate her and tells her it's just her imagination and that dreams should not be taken seriously. Here, she tells her lover of a terrible nightmare in which she is stabbed by an imaginary twin.

SARA: Do not accuse Heaven! It has left the imagination in our power. She is guided by our acts; and when these are in accordance with our duties and with virtue the imagination serves only to increase our peace and happiness. A single act, Mellefont, a single blessing bestowed upon us by a messenger of peace, in the name of the Eternal One, can restore my shattered imagination again. Do you still hesitate to do a few days sooner for love of me, what in any case you mean to do at some future time? Have pity on me, and consider that, although by this you may be freeing me only from torments of the imagination, yet these imagined torments are torments, and are real torments for her who feels them. Ah! could I but tell you the terrors of the last night half as vividly as I have felt them. Wearied with crying and grieving--my only occupations--I sank down on my bed with half-closed eyes. My nature wished to recover itself a moment, to collect new tears. But hardly asleep yet, I suddenly saw myself on the steepest peak of a terrible rock. You went on before, and I followed with tottering, anxious steps, strengthened now and then by a glance which you threw back upon me. Suddenly I heard behind me a gentle call, which bade me stop. It was my father's voice--I unhappy one, can I forget nothing which is his? Alas if his memory renders him equally cruel service; if he too cannot forget me!--But he has forgotten me. Comfort! Cruel comfort for his Sara!--But, listen, Mellefont! In turning round to this well--known voice, my foot slipped; I reeled, and was on the point of falling down the precipice, when just in time, I felt myself held back by one who resembled myself. I was just returning her my passionate thanks, when she drew a dagger from her bosom. "I saved you," she cried, "to ruin you!" She lifted her armed hand-- and--! I awoke with the blow. Awake, I still felt all the pain which a mortal stab must give, without the pleasure which it brings--the hope for the end of grief in the end of life.

SARA
by Gotthold Ephraim Lessing
translated by Ernest Bell

Marwood - 30s - England - 1755
Marwood, a woman wronged by Mellefont and the mother of his
child, schemes to win him back from the virtuous Sara. Here,
she drops her guise of a concerned relative for a brief moment
and we see that she is filled with self-loathing.

MARWOOD: *(Looking round.)* Am I alone? Can I take breath
again unobserved, and let the muscles of my face relax into their
natural position? I must just for a moment be the true Marwood in
all my features to be able again to bear the restraint of dissimulation!
How I hate thee, base dissimulation! Not because I love sincerity,
but because thou art the most pitiable refuge of powerless revenge.
I certainly would not condescend to thee, if a tyrant would lend me
his power or Heaven its thunderbolt.--Yet, if thou only servest my
end! The beginning is promising, and Mellefont seems disposed to
grow more confident. If my device succeeds and I can speak alone
with his Sara; then--yes, then, it is still very uncertain whether it
will be of any use to me. The truths about Mellefont will perhaps
be no novelty to her; and the calumnies she will perhaps not believe,
and the threats, perhaps, despise. But yet she shall hear truths,
calumnies and threats. It would be bad, if they did not leave any
sting at all in her mind. Silence; they are coming. I am no longer
Marwood, I am a worthless outcast, who tries by little artful tricks
to turn aside her shame--a bruised worm, which turns and fain would
wound at least the heel of him who trod upon it.

SEARCH AND DESTROY
by Howard Korder

Marie - 20s - U.S.A. - Present
A quiet receptionist proves that there's more to her than meets
the eye when she accepts an invitation to dinner with Martin
Mirkheim, a film producer. Marie tells Martin that she has
written a screenplay for a horror film and entertains him with a
rather bloody synopsis.

MARIE: Everybody's dead all over. Okay. She's caught. The
spinesucker has her pinned against the wall. With his other hand he
cracks open her boyfriend's head and smears his brains all over her
tits. Okay. The elevator's stuck between floors. This thing comes
out of him like a gangrene penis with a lobster claw and starts
burrowing into her. The pain's unbearable. Okay. Finally she
manages to reach the switch on the radial saw and rips it into him.
But he just smiles, okay, his stomach opens up and he absorbs it,
like he does and goes on pumping her up. She's gonna die, that's
all. *Except* inside him the saw's still going, spinning around, he
starts shaking and there's a, what do you, close shot, yeah, and the
saw rips out of his chest, there's this explosion of meat and pus
pouring out like from a fire hose, he climbs on her and tries to shove
the penis claw down her throat, okay, but she hacks it off with the
saw okay he goes shooting back against the glass door okay they
break he falls five floors, onto the metal spike in the fountain it goes
straight through his face, his brains spurt out and slide into the water
like fresh cum okay. He's dead, he's dead, he's finally fucking
dead. She walks away that's the end.

63

THE SECRET SITS IN THE MIDDLE
by Lisa-Marie Radano

Tina - 20s - Coney Island - Present

Tina is a young woman seeking an abortion. She is confronted by her sister, Angela, and her lover, Sonny, who both struggle to understand her decision. Tina lashes out at them and reveals that she feels responsible for her mother's death, and fears that she will eventually inflict the same pain on her own baby.

TINA: Then why'd she die and leave me Angela? *(to Mr. Runey)* Why'd she die so young, Mr. Poetic Loser? *(to Sonny)* You gonna get me an answer to that one by the enda today? Well, don't botha! *(to everyone)* I can tell you right now. She MADE herself sick because she was ANGRY. ANGRY she didn't do the thing she drempt of and worked for, so that undone thing became a chewing rat and had her for supper. And she said, eat. Eat. We hadda watch her skin turn grey and her hair fall out in chunks. When the rat ate her spine, they screwed her chin inta this contraption attached-ta her shoulders. They hadda have her upright so she could swallow alla the fucken pills lined up in fronta her like cadets. She'd say things--ask for a glass-a juice--but in her eyes she was already gone. Bastard doctors came and poked at her with cold tools and colder hands, not even bothering to draw the curtain for a woman's courtesy. I'll see them all in hell. They took everything the rat didn't take first. They fought over her body--here you take this, and she don't need that so I'll take it and pass the salt, until there was NOTHEN LEFT. NOTHEN of her ever bein a woman, so she said -hey life? SHOVE IT! She used ta be so beautiful. I'd sit on top-a the toilet and watch her put on her pink lipstick. She'd blot it and hand me the tissue smilen--a beautiful pink print-a her lips. Sometimes at night just as I'm driften off--I see her in her cocktail dress and evening pearls. She's reachen out the tissue with her kiss on it. I reach out for it but just when it touches me my heart falls offa tall building and lands like four separate pieces of heavy luggage. BOOM. BOOM. BOOM. BOOM. I wake up, sitting up, thinken I hate me. If it weren't for me she'd be alive and leapen around in a pastel tutu. Would you want that on you head? I'm never gonna have a baby. I'm never gonna do that to my baby.

64

THE SECRET SITS IN THE MIDDLE
by Lisa-Marie Radano

Angela - 20s-30s - Coney Island - Present
Tina can not bring herself to go through with the abortion and
she and Sonny leave to try and mend their relationship, leaving
Angela sitting with old Mr. Runey on a park bench. The two
discover that they both love "It's A Wonderful Life" and Angela
recalls a scene in the classic film that she will always remember.

ANGELA: My favorite part is in the drugstore, where Mary the
good and Violet the flirty both come to the soda fountain to visit
George. Mary gets there first. She's there twirlen on the stool--
stealthy...waiten. George's pals drop him off, whistlen and yellen
hee haw. George puts his hand on that old lighter and closes his
eyes. Wish I hadda million dollars. Mr. Gower yells at him for
bein late ta work. Vi comes scamperin in. Her bow is bigger than
Mary's but she's a good kid. "Hello Georgie!" Already Violet
knows how ta talk to a guy like he's wearen the first paira pants she
ever seen. "Hullo Mary," she says sullen. Mary's the enemy.
George says to Vi, "Two cents wortha shoelaces?" She's a regular.
While he's getten her the licorice, Violet sighs like a million
valentines. "I like him," she says. "You like alla the boys," says
Mary saucylike. Then Mr. Capra does this nice thing. He has Vi
say real innocent like, "What's wrong with that?" And what is? But
how often do they let-a cute blond in a movie get away with saying
something like this? Usually they stuff her through a meat grinder
or send her over the falls in a baggie. They don't punish Violet.
But George is for Mary, who sticks her tongue out as Vi leaves--just
as a reminder. Now she's got Georgie alone. He's maken her a
sundae and she's gazen at him with six different kindsa light while
he rails her for not desiren coconut and train travel and all other
exotic things he THINKS he wants. Mary just looks at him
knowing. The only important thing is George. The only important
thing is George. Some people just KNOW when they're on to the
right thing. Other people gotta struggle with oughta and mighta and

coulda, not seeing the perfect beauty-a what's right in fronta them. Mary knows this. She's nothen moren'a little kid in a flowered pinafore, but she's wise as-a dinosaur. She leans over while George is bent, and scooping out her ice cream and she whispers, "Is this your bad ear Georgie?" He don't hear. OK. So she leans in closer, her little face all dreamy and giddy wit love, and into his deaf ear with serious calm she whispers--"George Baily, I'll love you till the day I die." He don't hear. He don't even feel the soft little pieces-a her breath blowen against the hairs on his cheek. Life goes right on. This always kills me though. In this secret whisper of Mary's is everything you ever wanted to say to somebody after it was too late and they were gone. Every strong deep thing you ever wanted ta say ta someone but you were afraid ta hear what they'd say back. And every special message you wanted to shout out NOT to someone's ear, but to their SOUL! So that they could keep it forever known and wear it across their heart like a badge or a garland. George Bailey, I'll love you till the day I die. See how it stayed with him? And so did Mary. But only movies can do that.

SHIRLEY VALENTINE
by Willy Russell

Shirley Valentine - 42 - Greece - Present
Shirley vacations in Greece, leaving an empty life and loveless
marriage far behind in England. In Greece, she meets Costas,
a forward man who reawakens her sexuality. As she describes
Costas, it becomes evident.

SHIRLEY: Well that's when I met him. Y'know Christopher
Columbus. That's not his real name. His real name's Costas. But
I call him Christopher. Christopher Columbus. I'll bet y' don't
know why I call him that? It's because he's got a boat. Well, it's
his brother's boat actually. An because it's er--he, we--discovered
it. The island clitoris. I'm terrible, aren't I? I suppose y' think I'm
scandalous--a married woman, forty-two, got grown-up kids. I
suppose y' think I'm wicked. Jane does. "Shirley," she said,
"you're acting like a stupid teenager. I suppose the next think
you're going to tell me is that the earth trembled." "Trembled?" I
said. "Jane, I thought there's been an earthquake. It was at least
point nine on the Richter Scale." "Oh spare me the details," she's
goin', "spare me the details." Well she wasn't half jealous. But y'
see, it wasn't my fault; if she hadn't gone off, with the walkin'
groin, in the first place--I never would have met Christopher
Columbus. *(pause)* He kissed me stretch marks, y' know. He did.
He said--he said they were lovely...because they were a part of
me...an' I was lovely. He said--he said, stretch marks weren't to be
hidden away; they were to be displayed, to be proud of. He said my
stretch marks showed that I was alive, that I'd survived...that they
were marks of life. *(pause)* Aren't men full of shit? I mean, can
you imagine him, the mornin' after he's given me this speech--he
wakes up an' he finds *his* belly has got all these lines runnin' across
it? I mean, can y' see him? Rushin' to the mirror an' goin',
"Fantastic. Fuckin' fantastic. I've got stretch marks. At last!"

SWAN PLAY
by Elizabeth Egloff

Dora - 30s-50s - A House In Nebraska - Present
Dora is a nurse who has been married several times. Late one
night, a swan crashes into her window. As she nurses it back
to health, it metamorphasizes into a human male with whom she
develops a maternal then romantic relationship. Here she tells
the swan a strange tale of a man who once appeared at her door
and then just disappeared.

DORA: I am a great supporter of marriage, I don't think people are
meant to be alone. I don't think I am. Strange things happen to me
when I'm alone.
[SWAN: For example?]
DORA: Like things that are too private to talk about. Dangerous
things. Like my heart. And like once I was sitting here late at night
smoking a cigarette before I went to bed that was when I still
smoked cigarettes in fact that was when I still slept in the bedroom
ANYWAY I'm sitting here and I look up and I see a man standing
in the doorway of the bedroom. He looks like he just walked in
from the woods. He's covered with leaves and there is grass in his
hair and mud on his shoes. And he looks so sad and he looks so
much like Gerry only that was before I'd ever met Gerry so how
could he BUT there's something about him there's something in him
that's warm that's comfortable someplace I could ease my aching
heart and I think yes you're right love is the only thing that matters
if only I could get me some I could sleep again, I could eat again I
could belong to the world again, and just as I'm about to say Yes,
you're him You're the one, he quietly, without a word or a sign, he
quietly goes to the door and just, just, just, just, just...leaves.
[SWAN: Leaves.]
DORA: I never saw him again. It's always the way, isn't it? Some
people say I shouldn't marry so many, but I have to. They keep
disappearing on me. Turn around.

SWAN PLAY
by Elizabeth Egloff

Dora - 30s-50s - A House In Nebraska - Present
Dora and the swan often enjoy a game of checkers. While they play, Dora offers an amusing explanation for the behavior of men.

DORA: Do you think men are born on this planet? I don't think they are. I think men are born on the planet Pluto and they have them molecularly disassembled and radar-ed to the earth. Which is why. Which is why they are so, so, you have to take care of them in a very special way because they are foreign bodies being introduced to the system. And which is both why I love them and why I don't understand them whatever they're talking about.

I remember I met Gerry, you would think it was the day after he'd been radar-ed to the earth. There was something about Gerry. Something tender, something baby, like here was a man who needed more time to adapt to the eco-system. Gerry was always talking to himself. What is love and why do we do it? The day after we got married he went out in the woods and shot himself. The whole thing didn't exactly inspire my confidence. *(The swan moves for her. Then he moves for himself, jumping over another of her pieces, and stacking it on his side.)* Duane inspired my confidence, or what was left of it. Duane breathed life into a millimeter of myself, the piece of shrapnel I have come to regard as my heart. I took one look at Duane and said, Here's a man he doesn't ask questions, and he doesn't own a gun. Perfect, I thought, how could I go wrong? So I told him I loved him, and I loved myself. Duane said, How can you love me, if you don't love the world? Love the world, I said? I can hardly get out of bed. *(Then)* Two days later, he ran off. I was joking.

VITAL SIGNS
by Jane Martin

Waitress - 20s-30s - West Virginia - Present
This monologue, "Truck Stop," is presented by a spunky young woman who left her job as a nude waitress at a truck stop to hitch a ride across the country with a religious fanatic.

WAITRESS: Me? I waitressed at the only all-nude truck stop in West Virginia. It kinda caught on. We was all jaybird naked, cooks, cashiers, but girls, the bunch of us. We'd flip to see who worked the tables near the front door in December. Guy pulls a twelve-cylinder, 456-horsepower Detroit Diesel into the lot. Slides into my booth in a white silk suit with a tie with a diamond stud. Says he's the one, the only, Reverend Billy Frost, got him a sixteen wheel ministry an' the home phone number of the Holy Ghost. "Good evenin' little lady," he says, "I take you to be in the Garden of Eden or tied to the spokes of the wheel of fire. Now I'll have me a Decaf Cappucino and a side order of small curd cottage cheese, an' when I leave, Senorita, you're invited to ride." Slipped his silk coat over my shoulders, offered me his arm, walked me past the truckers to an all white rig, says "Resurrection Express" in letters of flame. "Climb up little lady," he says, "leave the dust of the road behind you." His eyes were serene as a hawk on an updraft, so I did.

Sang hymns, shouted scripture, and screwed me seven times on the way to Laramie, Wyoming. Left me by the side of the road at this deep pan pizza parlor run by two Koreans. Disappointed? Well, that's a real luxury in a life like mine, sailor. I got to generally trust any human being ain't armed or got blood on their shoes. Tell you what. Buy me a beer and give me a ride into Palm Springs, you can tell me your modus operandi.

70

VITAL SIGNS
by Jane Martin

A Lover - Any Age - Any Place - Any Time
A love affair is heading for disaster as is here evidenced by the fact that one lover has reached the point where she can no longer stand the sounds her partner makes in "Sounds You Make."

LOVER: There's a very particular sound I associate with you. Just the smallest exhalation of breath. So light sometimes it's just on the edge of being heard. But you mean me to hear it. It's not spontaneous or surprised. It's meant to wound. It's meant to delicately remind me of my unreason. It intimates something soiled and hopelessly emotional. That you by all rights should disdain or reject in me but at the same time it makes you unassailably good because all you do is make the sound and that resigned, fluttering palms up gesture and stay reasonably silent in the face of what, if you did speak, you might call my <u>provocations</u>. And every time you do it, I fell vaguely ashamed because <u>I</u> haven't been good, <u>I</u> haven't been accepting or forgiving or forebearing. I've had the immense bad taste to feel something when you didn't instigate it, or ask for it or, worse yet, simply weren't in the mood for it. And the worst of it is that it's so painfully clear how much you enjoy what you're feeling about me and how you want me to hear you feeling it. So that I realize that now what used to be my pleasure in your company has become this longing to never, never, never hear you make that sound again. Never. Never.

71

WOMAN FROM THE TOWN
by Samm-Art Williams

Laura - 47 - North Carolina - December 22-25, Present
Laura is a determined woman who has devoted her life to working the family farm. Her sister, Lila, has returned to the farm at Christmas for a visit and Laura reveals her resentment of Lila's choice to live in the city by reminding her that she has spent her life behind a plow and battling the banks with no thanks from her family.

LAURA: My sister Lila's still got nerves made out of cast iron. Walking up the road like the conquering hero come home. Never thought she'd do it. Coming home with a bastard young'n. *(She crosses SR onto porch to SR porch railing and looks at the fields.)* Well, they won't find a pot of gold at the end of this rainbow. Just buckets of my sweat out there in them fields. Foot tubs full of my tears when they all started leaving and...dying out. *(She crosses to SL on porch.)* So don't come back here bringing me no sympathy cards. *(She throws the letter on the floor SL of porch steps.)* Dirt under my fingernails. Hands with rope marks on them...from plowing. Combines taking over everything. Folks selling out. Banks taking over what the big combines don't want. *(She crosses to rocker and sits.)* Choking the small farmer. Turning us into farm house dinosaurs. State Governor lies so bad I don't know if it come natural or he trained for it. Governor made me destroy my television the other night. I threw a hammer through the screen trying to hit him. Told us he wanted to help the ones in need. Soon as I heard the lie...I killed by television. But he kept right on talking. *(Looking SL at Lila and Rita.)* I didn't pick you up from the bus station. That ought to tell you how bad I want you back here. *(She stands looking SL.)* You waited too long, Lila. It's too late. So don't bring me no sympathy cards. *(She sits in rocker and picks up basket, continues decorating it.)* We used to have so much fun at holiday time. Warmth all around. Our favorite time of the year. The Wilson sisters. *(She hums "Silent Night, Holy Night".)* That was a long time ago. It would take you to fuck up my Christmas. *(Laura closes her eyes and rocks.)*

72

WOMAN FROM THE TOWN
by Samm-Art Williams

Laura - 47 - North Carolina - December 22-25, Present
Here, Laura mourns the loss of her femininity. Years of hard
work on the farm have taken their toll on her body - but not on
her spirit.

LAURA: I wish I could love you, sister. But I spent too many days
shelling peas, feeding hogs, chopping cotton, and plowing. Plowing
and walking them long hot rows for so long that sometimes I thought
I was a mule. Just me and my boy. *(Replaces picture on table.)*
Lila, she's living the high life. I look at my hands sometimes and
I want to just scream. Underneath these calluses are soft, warm
hands that need to be held. Scars and scratches on arms that need
to embrace. There's a woman inside these overalls. *(Rises.)* A
woman--no, a lady, damn it!! *(Works area.)* Working! Chopping!
Plowing! Pulling! Pulling! Gee to the left mule! Haw to the right!
New giddy-up! Giddy-up, I say. Got to stay straight between the
row. Dirt in my shoes. Hot sun burning and blistering skin that
should be smooth as brown satin. Screams and screeches that should
be soft blues notes played by my hands. Would you like to waltz,
Laura? Certainly, Sir. *(Picks up Lila's scarf and dances a little.)*
My perfume? I'm glad you like it. Waiter, champagne for my
glass. Hell, I can dream, can't I? Because there's a lady underneath
these overalls...a lady that I'll never find again.

WOMAN FROM THE TOWN
by Samm-Art Williams

Hazel - 58 - North Carolina - December 22-25, Present
Lila has come to town with the express purpose of buying distressed farms whose mortgages are overdue. Hazel is a neighbor of Laura's and one of those desperate to keep their homes. Here she begs Lila to allow her to keep her land, for she hopes that one day her sons - who have left the farm for more lucrative jobs elsewhere - will return to work the land.

HAZEL: All you can do is raise them. They can't stay babies forever. Sometimes you pray to God, "Don't let them grow past twelve 'cause I know they gonna leave me. Let me hold on just a while longer." You look out across the fields and you see them running barefoot. Chasing a rabbit and kicking up dust. Laughter and happiness coming from their little sunburned lips. And just that fast, they're gone and it's all changed. Just that fast. I can't believe I've ever been happy. I can't remember that far back. And I know now, God, that it's just between me and you. I musta done something powerful mean against you, 'cause I'm feeling the full blast of your curse. Whatever it was, I want you to know that I'm sorry. But...but...if you can...let me see my boys running across them fields again. While the soil is still mine. If you got more curses for me...I'll take them. Whatever you think I oughta have, 'cause you got the upper hand. But land and babies is all we got. Let me keep one of them...please. If it's Conway, it's all right. If it's Wayne, it's all right. But let me hear one of their voices running happily across the dust fields, while the soil is still mine...just once before I die. Amen.

ZARA SPOOK AND OTHER LURES
by Joan Ackermann-Blount

Margery - 20s-30s - Southwest - Present

Margery is vacationing in the Southwest. She has hitched a ride with Mel. To pass the time in the car, Margery shares a childhood memory with Mel that she hopes will spark a conversation.

MARGERY: Driving at night can be so hypnotic, don't you think? As if the road were driving us. Funny, fate. Perfect strangers sharing a journey, perhaps the three most important hours of our life. What is it that's pulling us toward it, beyond the headlights out there. Some remnant from our past, some piece of ourselves.

[MEL: You sound like that fellow from the Twilight Zone.]

MARGERY: *(Laughs)* I know I probably sound ridiculous. It just always seems curious to me what it is that makes people choose the disastrous courses they do. I mean, look at me right now. What was it that made me ask you for a ride at the airport? You could be a mass murderer for all I know. Isn't it odd how you can open up to a total stranger, share things you would never tell anyone else, knowing you'll never see that person again. I feel very close to you right now. Ask me something personal, I'll tell you anything. Go ahead. Let me give you something of value, something intimate.

[MEL: I don't know, m'am...]

MARGERY: Please. Go ahead, you'll be doing me a kindness.

[MEL: Intimate? You mean, physical?]

MARGERY: I know what I'll tell you, I've never told this to anyone before. Ha, I can't believe I'm telling you this. When I was twelve my Aunt Clair took it upon herself to inform me of the facts of life. I don't know why but she began the conversation by telling me about her heart murmur. For some reason I mixed it all up and for the longest time I thought that an orgasm was something that happened in your heart. Isn't that a remarkable idea? Really? You can imagine how confused I was later on. *(Pause)* There, now you know something about me that no one else knows. *(Pause)* Don't you think it's actually quite poetic? An involuntary stirring in the heart? *(Pause)* So. *(Pause)* Is there any more coca-cola left? My throat's gone dry.

ZARA SPOOK AND OTHER LURES
by Joan Ackermann-Blount

Ramona - 30s - Southwest - Present
Ramona is Mel's estranged wife. Besides discussing her rather dangerous husband, her life's passion is fishing. While participating in a fishing tournament, Ramona is bitten by a rattlesnake that she suspects was placed in her boat by Mel. While waiting for help to arrive, she discusses Mel's inability to express emotions.

RAMONA: That's what I'm trying to tell you. The man has good hands. If only he could have talked to me. I mean, I had cryosurgery on my cervix after a bad pap smear? And he couldn't say one word to me about it. Not one related word. He waited out in the parking lot, I got in the car and the first thing he said after ten minutes driving home was he didn't know why everybody complained so much about the new Coca-Cola formula he liked it.
[EVELYN: He likes the new Coca-Cola formula?]
RAMONA: He had a nephew Hardy, favorite nephew, loved him like a son, he died, drowned in less than two feet of water, drunk as a skunk. He was so busted up inside you could hear the pieces break apart. Think we could sit around and cry together, share memories, visit with Hardy's folks? That man sat for two days in his truck, parked up on the mesa, wouldn't eat, wouldn't talk, wouldn't go to the funeral or the cook-out.
[EVELYN: Must have hurt something awful.]
RAMONA: I slept out in the back of the truck, waiting for him to come and talk to me. Saw three UFOs. Nearly froze to death. He never came back, never said a word about it. Listen to this. I had an affair with someone, told him about it, he just stood there and stared at me, stared like I wasn't even there, like I'd evaporated. I could see my reflection in his eyes. The opposite of tears.

ZORA NEALE HURSTON
by Laurence Holder

Zora Neale Hurston - 40s-60s - Bus Station, NY - 1950s
Zora Neale Hurston introduces herself to the audience as an outspoken black writer who has studied with Alain Locke and collaborated with Langston Hughes. She has fallen on bad times, but doesn't seem full of regret as she remembers her childhood and early education.

ZORA: My Gawd! Look at this place. Some old dumpy looking bus station. They calls this a waiting room but they couldn't mean it. It's dreary, dirty. And to think, I used to be somebody in the big time. Books lining bookshelves three feet deep and twelve feet high.

But that was a long time ago. Now I'm heading back to Boca Raton. That's in Florida. I could tell you where it is, but I'm not looking forward to visitors right in through here. I mean, I have been in it up to my elbows and I can tell you a thing or two about people's inhumanity. How can a man look at someone and decide he knows all there is about that person. Like just a moment ago with that ticket clerk.

Now this man is going to give me a hard time because he can't find where and what time for the bus to Boca Raton. He's searching and cussing and I sympathize with him, it being Christmas Eve and all, but even that isn't my fault. He's testy when he finally finds it in his black book, and then he tells me it's $29.25. I only got 29 dollars. Period. He swears that I got to pay the whole fare or his management and union's gonna come down here and declare war against me. Me! Zora Neale Hurston, a woman who has never cowtailed to anybody, anyplace, anywhere. I may look like a waif, but I have walked with kings and queens. I was the queen of the Harlem Renaissance.

Anyway, he wished me a Merry Christmas, then he give me that ticket. *(Music--Flute)*

I was always the sassy girl from de muck, de basin, de

77

bottom. That's where civilization ends and living begins. The girl from Eatonville, Florida, the first colored town to incorporate in America. The first town built and governed by Negroes. In our yard we had a swing and an oak tree. My daddy was the town preacher and he would preach underneath that tree. My mama sang in the choir, and they both told stories. They could tell the tail off a monkey if they had a mind to. I know, cause I've done it quite a few times myself, and they taught me.

Maybe it all began when Mama died when I was nine. I was definitely Mama's girl and when Daddy went and married another woman who just couldn't get along with me nor me with her, then I had to go live with relatives, and they never understood me so they mistreated me. But that didn't bother me none. I made my peace with the universe real quick and accepted the challenge of responsibility.

When I was fourteen, I just up and joined a Gilbert and Sullivan travelling dramatic troupe--as a maid. I had a little money, and what was more important, I had myself a place to stay. Not much of a place, but still it was my place. It helped me go to night school and get ready for college.

And suddenly, there I am in Washington, D.C., the capital of these magnificent United States. And I'm going to Howard University, the all-cullud school, the mecca for all the important Negro scholarship going on in the country.

ZORA NEALE HURSTON
by Laurence Holder

Zora Neale Hurston - 40s-60s - New York City - Late 1920s
Zora's genius for combining the traditional elements of folklore
with difficult contemporary issues is seen here in her tale of the
origins of the power struggle between men and women.

ZORA: Zora Neale Hurston, Second Prize Winner for Fiction. I'm
gonna tell y'all one of my little stories.

In the beginning, God created man and woman, yes he did.
And he put 'em together to live in a house. Back in them days, they
was even balanced, see. They used to do the same things, and
neither one of them had more strength than the other. Well, suh, the
man got tired of this, yes he did, so he decided he'd go on up to
Heaven and ask God. So he went up to Heaven and he asked God
to give him more strength than the woman, so he could make the
woman mind. So God gave it to him. So he's so happy, he ran
down all the steps of Heaven till he got home. And he got home,
and he's beating his chest and he said, "Woman! Here's your boss.
God done told me you got to do everything I tell you to do." Well,
the woman got mad, so she tried to fight him. The first time, he
beat her. She couldn't fight him. So she tried again. She still
couldn't fight him. She tried a third time. She couldn't fight him.
Every time, he'd outdo her, overpower her. So the woman got mad
and she decided to go up to Heaven. She went up to Heaven and
said, "God! How come you give the man more strength than me?"
And God said, "the man has as much power as he always had."

"But how come he can beat me, then? He never could beat
me before."

"Well, the man come up to me, and he asked me to give him
more strength, and I give it to him."

"Well, God, give me more strength."

"I can't do that. The man asked me first, and what I give,
I can't take back."

So the woman got mad, and she went to the Devil, yes she
did. And the Devil said, "I want you to go back up to Heaven, and
I want you to get the three keys that God got on his mantlepiece.

ZORA NEALE HURSTON

Then I want you to bring me them three keys, and I'm gonna tell you what to do with 'em." So she went up to Heaven and she got the three keys. And she came down to Hell, and the Devil said, "You see this first key? This is the key to the kitchen. Now you know how a man favors his stomach. See this second key? This is the key to the bedroom. You know a man don't like to be locked out of that either. And this third key is the key to the Generations. Now I want you to go home and I want you to lock up all three doors. And don't open any door till that man uses his strength for your benefit and your favor. Oh yeah, and don't you talk too much about it either. As a matter of fact, don't you tell him nothing at all." So the woman went home and locked up the three doors. She was just sitting out there, sitting on the porch, just a-rockin' herself and enjoying the sun, and the man come home. He see the three doors is locked. He said, "Woman, who locked these three doors?"

"I did."

"Well, where did you get the key?"

"God give me the key."

So the man went up to Heaven and said, "God! You give the woman the three keys?"

God said, "Yes, I did."

"Well, Lord give me the three keys."

"I can't do that. She asked me first and what I give I can't take back."

"Well, how I'm gonna get to the bedroom? How I'm gonna get to my Generations? How I'm gonna get to the kitchen?"

"Go and ask the woman."

So the man went on down the steps of Heaven all humble now, you know, and he went home and he tried to make a deal with the woman. He said, "Sweetheart, honey, I'll tell you what I'll do. I'll give you half my strength if you'll just let me hold on to the three keys." And the woman was just about to give him the keys when the Devil come. And the Devil said, "Stop! Don't you let those keys out your hand. You hold onto those keys."

So you men think you walking all around with all your strength, but it's the woman who holds the keys.

PERMISSIONS ACKNOWLEDGMENTS

Grateful acknowledgment is made for permission to reprint excerpts from the following plays:

AMULETS AGAINST THE DRAGON FORCES by Paul Zindel. Copyright © 1989 by Paul Zindel. Reprinted by permission of the author's agent, Wiley Hausam, International Creative Management, Inc., 40 West 57th Street, New York, NY 10019. Published by Dramatists Play Service, Inc.

A MURDER OF CROWS by Ed Graczyk. Copyright © 1989 by Ed Graczyk. Reprinted by permission of the author's agent, Mitch Douglas, International Creative Management, Inc., 40 West 57th Street, New York, NY 10019. Published by Samuel French, Inc.

APOCALYPTIC BUTTERFLIES by Wendy MacLeod. Copyright © 1990 by Wendy MacLeod. Reprinted by permission of the author's agent, Helen Merrill, Ltd. CAUTION: Professionals and amateurs are hereby warned that APOCALYPTIC BUTTERFLIES is fully protected under the Copyright Laws of the United States of America, the British Commonwealth, including the Dominion of Canada, and all other countries of the International Copyright Union and Universal Copyright Convention, and are subject to royalty. All rights, including professional, amateur, motion picture, recitation, lecturing, public reading, radio and television broadcasting and the rights of translation into foreign languages are strictly reserved. Particular emphasis is laid on the question of readings, permission for which must be secured from the author's agent in writing. All inquiries concerning the amateur and professional production rights to APOCALYPTIC BUTTERFLIES by WENDY MACLEOD should be addressed to the author's agent, Helen Merrill, Ltd., 435 West 23rd Street, Suite 1A, New York, NY 10011, USA. No amateur performance of any of the plays may be given without obtaining, in advance, the written permission of Helen Merrill, Ltd. All inquiries concerning rights (other than production rights) should also be addressed to Helen Merrill, Ltd. Published by Dramatists Play Service, Inc.

APPLES by Ian Dury. Copyright © 1989 by Ian Dury. Reprinted by permission of Faber and Faber, Ltd., 3 Queen Square, London WC1N 3AU, England.

AT THE STILL POINT by Jordan Roberts. Copyright © 1990 by Jordan Roberts. Reprinted by permission of the author. AT THE STILL POINT was first produced by: PRIMARY STAGES, New York, Casey Childs, Artistic Director, at the William Redfield Theater, April 1990.

AUGUST SNOW by Reynolds Price. Copyright © 1989 by Reynolds Price. Reprinted by permission of the author's agent, Harriet Wasserman, 137 East 36th Street, New York, NY 10016.

BELLES by Mark Dunn. Copyright © 1989 by Mark Dunn. Reprinted by permission of Samuel French, Inc., 45 West 25th Street, New York, NY 10010.

PERMISSIONS ACKNOWLEDGMENTS

BRILLIANT TRACES by Cindy Lou Johnson. Copyright © 1989 by Cindy Lou Johnson. Reprinted by permission of the author's agent, George P. Lane, William Morris Agency, 1350 Avenue of the Americas, New York, NY 10019. Published by Dramatists Play Service, Inc.

DEMON WINE by Thomas Babe. Copyright © 1989 by Thomas Babe. Reprinted by permission of the author. Published by Dramatists Play Service, Inc.

EACH DAY DIES WITH SLEEP by José Rivera. Copyright © 1989 by José Rivera. Reprinted by permission of the author's agent, Wiley Hausam, International Creative Management, Inc., 40 West 57th Street, New York, NY 10019.

ELLIOT LOVES by Jules Feiffer. Copyright © 1990 by Jules Feiffer. Reprinted by permission of the author's agent, Robert Lantz, The Lantz Office, 888 Seventh Avenue, New York, NY 10106 and The Grove Press, 841 Broadway, New York, NY 10003.

THE FILM SOCIETY by Jon Robin Baitz. Copyright © 1989 by Available Light Productions, Inc. Reprinted by permission of the author's agent, George P. Lane, William Morris Agency, 1350 Avenue of the Americas, New York, NY 10019. Published by Samuel French, Inc.

FLORIDA GIRLS by Nancy Hasty. Copyright © 1981 by Nancy Hasty. Reprinted by permission of the author's agent, Richard Krawetz, Agency for the Performing Arts, 888 7th Avenue, New York, New York 10106, all rights reserved.

GAL BABY by Sandra Deer. Copyright © 1990 by Sandra Deer. Reprinted by permission of the author.

GOD'S COUNTRY by Steven Dietz. Copyright © 1988, 1990 by Steven John Dietz. Reprinted by permission of the author's agent, Wiley Hausam, International Creative Management, Inc., 40 West 57th Street, New York, NY 10019. Published by Samuel French, Inc.

IMAGINING BRAD by Peter Hedges. Copyright © 1988, 1989, 1990 by Peter Hedges. Reprinted by permission of the author's agent, Jeannine Edmunds, Curtis Brown, Ltd., Ten Astor Place, New York, NY 10003.

IS HE STILL DEAD? by Donald Freed. Copyright © 1990 by Donald Freed. Reprinted by permission of the author's agent: Stephen Lisk, c/o ICM, 8899 Beverly Blvd., Los Angeles, CA 90048. Published by Broadway Play Publishing, Inc., 357 West 20th Street, New York, NY 10011.

KURU by Josh C. Manheimer. Copyright © 1990 by J.C. Manheimer & Co., Ltd. Reprinted by permission of the author and Graham Agency, New York. CAUTION: Professionals and amateurs are hereby warned that

82

PERMISSIONS ACKNOWLEDGMENTS

KURU is subject to royalty. It is fully protected under the copyright laws of the United States of America, and of all countries covered by the International Copyright Union (including Canada and the British Commonwealth), and of all countries covered by the Pan-American Copyright Convention and the Universal Copyright Convention, and of all countries with which the United States has reciprocal copyright relations. All rights, including professional, amateur, motion picture, recitation, lecturing, public reading, radio broadcasting, television, audio and video recording, and the rights of translation into foreign languages are strictly reserved. All inquiries concerning rights should be addressed to Graham Agency, 311 West 43rd Street, New York, New York 10036.

LETTICE & LOVAGE by Peter Shaffer. Copyright © 1987, 1990 by Venticelli, Inc. Reprinted by permission of the Lantz Office, 888 Seventh Avenue, New York, NY 10106. Published by Harper and Row, Publishers, 10 East 53rd Street, New York, NY 10022.

THE MAGIC ACT by Laurence Klavan. Copyright © 1989 by Laurence Klavan. Reprinted by permission of the Tantleff Office, 375 Greenwich Street, Suite 700, New York, NY 10013. Originally produced at Ensemble Studio Theatre, New York City, Curt Dempster, Artistic Director. Published by Dramatists Play Service, Inc.

MAIDS OF HONOR by Joan Casademont. Reprinted by permission of the author and The Gersh Agency, 130 West 42nd Street, New York, NY 10036.

MARY AND LIZZIE by Frank McGuinness. Copyright © 1989 by Frank McGuinness. Reprinted by permission of Faber and Faber, Ltd., 3 Queen Square, London WC1N 3AU, England.

MIRIAM'S FLOWERS by Migdalia Cruz. Copyright © 1990 by Migdalia Cruz. Reprinted by permission of the author's agent, Peregrine Whittlesey, 345 East 80th Street, New York, NY 10021. This play was developed by INTAR's playwrights' lab under the direction of Maria Irene Fornes, the Mark Taper Forum's New Play Festival, Midwest PlayLabs and Playwrights Horizons.

MORE FUN THAN BOWLING by Steven Dietz. Copyright © 1985, 1990 by Steven Jon Dietz. Reprinted by permission of the author's agent, Wiley Hausam, International Creative Management, Inc., 40 West 57th Street, New York, NY 10019. Published by Samuel French, Inc.

QUEEN OF THE LEAKY ROOF CIRCUIT by Jimmy Breslin. Copyright © 1990 by Jimmy Breslin. Reprinted by permission of the author's agent, Barry Weiner, Artists Agency, 230 West 55th Street, Suite 29D, New York, NY 10019.

SANTIAGO by Manuel Pereiras [García]. Copyright © 1986, 1989, 1990 by Manuel Pereiras [García]. Reprinted by permission of the author. This play was written during the 1985-1986 INTAR'S Hispanic Playwrights-in-Residence Workshop, directed by María Irene

83

PERMISSIONS ACKNOWLEDGMENTS

Fornés, who directed the play for a mini-workshop production at that Theatre as well as doing the dramaturgy. The play received another workshop production at Circle Repertory Lab, co-sponsored by The Blue Heron Theater, and it had its world premiere at the Wilma Theatre in Philadelphia, both directed by Robert F. Furhmann. *Santiago* is dedicated to Migdalia Cruz.

SARA by Gotthold Ephraim Lessing, translated by Ernest Bell. Extracts from SARA by Gotthold Lessing, published by Absolute Press, Bath, England. Reprinted by permission of Absolute Press.

SEARCH AND DESTROY by Howard Korder. Copyright © 1988 by Howard Korder. Reprinted by permission of the author and The Tantleff Office, 375 Greenwich Street, Suite 700, New York, NY 10013.

THE SECRET SITS IN THE MIDDLE by Lisa-Marie Radano. Copyright © 1988 by Lisa-Marie Radano. Reprinted by permission of the author.

SHIRLEY VALENTINE by Willy Russell. Reprinted by permission of Methuen London, Michelin House, 81 Fulham Road, London SW3 6RB, England.

SWAN PLAY by Elizabeth Egloff. Copyright © 1989 by Elizabeth Egloff. Reprinted by permission of the author and The Gersh Agency, 130 West 42nd Street, New York, NY 10036.

VITAL SIGNS by Jane Martin. Copyright © 1990 by Alexander Speer, as trustee. All rights reserved. CAUTION: Professionals and amateurs are hereby warned that "Sounds You Make" and "Truck Stop" from Jane Martin's <u>Vital Signs</u>, being fully protected under the copyright laws of the United States of America, the British Commonwealth, including the dominion of Canada, and all other countries of the International Copyright Union and the Universal Copyright Convention, is subject to royalty. All rights, including professional, amateur, motion picture, recitation, lecturing, public reading, radio and television broadcasting, and the rights of translation into foreign languages, are strictly reserved. Particular emphasis is laid on the question of reading, permission for which must be secured from the author's agent in writing. All inquiries concerning rights should be addressed to the author's representative, Samuel French, Inc., at 45 West 25th Street, New York, NY 10010.

WOMAN FROM THE TOWN by Samm-Art Williams. Copyright © 1990 by Samm-Art Williams. Reprinted by permission of the author. Published by Samuel French, Inc.

ZARA SPOOK AND OTHER LURES by Joan Ackermann-Blount. Copyright © 1989 by Joan Ackermann-Blount. Reprinted by permission of the author and the author's agent, Mary Harden, Bret Adams, Ltd., 448 West 44th Street, New York, NY 10036.

84

PERMISSIONS ACKNOWLEDGMENTS

ZORA NEALE HURSTON by Laurence Holder. Copyright © 1989 by Lawrence Holder. Reprinted by permission of the author and the author's agent, Lawrence Jordan Literary Agency, 250 West 57th Street, Room 1527, New York, NY 10107.

For up-to-date information on unpublished plays, send an SASE to Smith and Kraus, Inc., Main Street, P.O. Box 10, Newbury, VT 05051.